GOD'S
ANSWERS
for LIFE'S
QUESTIONS

GOD'S
ANSWERS
for LIFE'S
QUESTIONS

BETHANYHOUSE
Minneapolis, Minnesota

God's Answers for Life's Questions
Copyright © 1998, 2011
Bethany House Publishers

Pages 318–320 are a continuation of the copyright page.

Originally published in four volumes by Albury Publishing:
    God's Answers for Your Every Question
    God's Answers for Your Every Question, for Mothers
    God's Answers for Your Every Question, for Fathers
    God's Answers for Your Every Question, for Students
This volume has been condensed and revised.

Cover design by Eric Walljasper

Published by Bethany House Publishers
11400 Hampshire Avenue South
Bloomington, Minnesota 55438

Bethany House Publishers is a division of
Baker Publishing Group, Grand Rapids, Michigan.

Printed in the United States of America

ISBN 978-0-7642-0864-5

Contents

What Is the Secret to Good Relationships?

As a Young Person, I Have Some Questions About Relationships

Can You Help Me With These Challenges?

HOW CAN
I KNOW YOU,
GOD?

So much has changed since the Bible was written. How can I be sure its answers still apply to my life today?

Even if it was written in Scripture long ago, you can be sure it's written for us.

ROMANS 15:4 THE MESSAGE

I tell you the truth, until heaven and earth disappear, not the smallest letter, not the least stroke of a pen, will by any means disappear from the Law until everything is accomplished.

MATTHEW 5:18 NIV

People are like grass; their beauty is like a flower in the field. The grass withers and the flower fades. But the word of the Lord remains forever.

1 PETER 1:24–25 NLT

Every part of Scripture is God-breathed and useful one way or another—showing us truth, exposing our rebellion, correcting our mistakes, training us to live God's way.

2 TIMOTHY 3:16 THE MESSAGE

The word of God is living and powerful.

HEBREWS 4:12 NKJV

They are not just idle words for you—they are your life.

DEUTERONOMY 32:47 NIV

— PRAYERS —

Open my eyes to see the wonderful truths in your instructions.

PSALM 119:18 NLT

Your eternal word, O Lord, stands firm in heaven. Your faithfulness extends to every generation, as enduring as the earth you created. Your regulations remain true to this day, for everything serves your plans.

PSALM 119:89–91 NLT

From studying your laws, I found out long ago that you made them to last forever. . . . All you say can be trusted; your teachings are true and will last forever.

PSALM 119:152, 160 CEV

— PROMISES —

The instructions of the Lord are perfect, reviving the soul. The decrees of the Lord are trustworthy, making wise the simple. The commandments of the Lord are right, bringing joy to the heart. The commands of the

Lord are clear, giving insight for living. . . . The laws of the Lord are true; each one is fair. They are more desirable than gold, even the finest gold. They are sweeter than honey, even honey dripping from the comb. They are a warning to your servant, a great reward for those who obey them.

PSALM 19:7–11 NLT

[Jesus said,] Heaven and earth will pass away, but My words will not pass away.

MATTHEW 24:35 NASB

I believe in God and I go to church. Is that enough, or is there more?

"Men, what is it necessary for me to do that I may be saved?" And they answered, "Believe in and on the Lord Jesus Christ [give yourself up to Him, take yourself out of your own keeping and entrust yourself into His keeping] and you will be saved."

ACTS 16:30–31 AMP

Jesus replied, "I tell you the truth, unless you are born again, you cannot see the Kingdom of God." "What do you mean?" exclaimed Nicodemus. "How can an old man go back into his mother's womb and be born again?" Jesus replied, "I assure you, no one can enter the Kingdom of God without being born of water and the Spirit. Humans can reproduce only human life, but the Holy Spirit gives birth to spiritual life."

JOHN 3:3–6 NLT

For God so greatly loved and dearly prized the world that He [even] gave up His only-begotten (unique) Son, so that whoever believes in (trusts, clings to, relies on) Him shall not perish (come to destruction, be lost) but have eternal (everlasting) life.

JOHN 3:16 AMP

Anyone who trusts in him is acquitted; anyone who refuses to trust him has long since been under the death sentence without knowing it. And why? Because of that person's failure to believe in the one-of-a-kind Son of God when introduced to him.

JOHN 3:18 THE MESSAGE

And all who trust him—God's Son—to save them have eternal life.

JOHN 3:36 TLB

For if you do not believe that I am He [Whom I claim to be—if you do not adhere to, trust in, and rely on Me], you will die in your sins.

JOHN 8:24 AMP

*Jesus, I want to
believe in you.
How can I be sure
you are real?*

You will seek Me, inquire for, and require Me [as a vital necessity] and find Me when you search for Me with all your heart. I will be found by you, says the Lord.

JEREMIAH 29:13–14 AMP

For everyone who asks receives, and he who seeks finds, and to him who knocks it will be opened.

MATTHEW 7:8 NASB

All who seek the Lord will praise him. Their hearts will rejoice with everlasting joy.

PSALM 22:26 NLT

The person who has My commands and keeps them is the one who [really] loves Me; and whoever [really] loves Me will be loved by My Father, and I [too] will love him and will show (reveal, manifest) Myself to him. [I will let Myself be clearly seen by him and make Myself real to him.]

JOHN 14:21 AMP

— INSTRUCTIONS —

Before you trust, you have to listen. But unless Christ's Word is preached, there's nothing to listen to.

ROMANS 10:17 THE MESSAGE

For what I received I passed on to you as of first importance: that Christ died for our sins according to the Scriptures, that he was buried, that he was raised on the third day according to the Scriptures, and that he appeared to Peter, and then to the Twelve. After that, he appeared to more than five hundred of the brothers at the same time.

1 CORINTHIANS 15:3–6 NIV

To these He also presented Himself alive after His suffering, by many convincing proofs, appearing to them over a period of forty days and speaking of the things concerning the kingdom of God.

ACTS 1:3 NASB

There are also many other things that Jesus did, which if they were written one by one, I suppose that even the world itself could not contain the books that would be written.

JOHN 21:25 NKJV

These have been written so that you may believe that Jesus is the Christ, the Son of God; and that believing you may have life in His name.

JOHN 20:31 NASB

For you know that God paid a ransom to save you from the empty life you inherited from your ancestors. And the ransom he paid was not mere gold or silver. It was the precious blood of Christ, the sinless, spotless Lamb of God. God chose him as your ransom long before the world began, but he has now revealed him to you in these last days.

Through Christ you have come to trust in God. And you have placed your faith and hope in God because he raised Christ from the dead and gave him great glory. . . .

For you have been born again, but not to a life that will quickly end. Your new life will last forever because it comes from the eternal, living word of God.

1 PETER 1:18–21, 23 NLT

Can you imagine the breathtaking recovery life makes, sovereign life, in those who grasp with both hands this wildly extravagant life-gift, this grand setting-everything-right, that the one man Jesus Christ provides? Here it is in a nutshell: Just as one person [Adam] did it wrong and got us in all this trouble with sin and death, another person [Christ] did it right and got us out of it. But more than just getting us out of trouble, he got us into life!

ROMANS 5:17-18 THE MESSAGE

— PROMISES —

He is real and . . . he rewards those who truly want to find him.

HEBREWS 11:6 NCV

No one's ever seen or heard anything like this, never so much as imagined anything quite like it—what God has arranged for those who love him. But you've seen and heard it because God by his Spirit has brought it all out into the open before you. . . .

We didn't learn this by reading books or going to school; we learned it from God, who taught us person-to-person through Jesus, and we're passing it on to you in the same firsthand, personal way.

The unspiritual self, just as it is by nature, can't receive the gifts of God's Spirit. There's no capacity for them. They seem like so much silliness. Spirit can be known only by spirit—God's Spirit and our spirits in open communion.

1 CORINTHIANS 2:9, 13–15 THE MESSAGE

God once said, "Let the light shine out of the darkness!" This is the same God who made his light shine in our hearts by letting us know the glory of God that is in the face of Christ.

2 CORINTHIANS 4:6 NCV

— PRAYERS —

I pray for you constantly, asking God, the glorious Father of our Lord Jesus Christ, to give you wisdom to see clearly and really understand who Christ is and all that he has done for you. I pray that your hearts will be flooded with light so that you can see something of the future he has called you to share. . . . I pray that you will begin to understand how incredibly great his power is to help those who believe him.

EPHESIANS 1:16–19 TLB

Hear my voice when I call, O Lord; be merciful to me and answer me. My heart says of you, "Seek his face!" Your face, Lord, I will seek.

PSALM 27:7–8 NIV

— EXAMPLE —

Thomas, one of the Twelve, said he had to see for himself that Jesus was alive (see John 20:24–25):

[Jesus appeared and] said to Thomas, "Put your finger here; see my hands. Reach out your hand and put it into my side. Stop doubting and believe." Thomas said to him, "My Lord and my God!"

JOHN 20:27–28 NIV

Jesus said, "So, you believe because you've seen with your own eyes. Even better blessings are in store for those who believe without seeing."

JOHN 20:29 THE MESSAGE

Is there something I need to do to begin a relationship with you, Lord? Where do I start?

Salvation that comes from trusting Christ is already within easy reach. In fact, the Scriptures say,

If you confess with your mouth that Jesus is Lord and believe in your heart that God raised him from the dead, you will be saved. For it is by believing in your heart that you are made right with God, and it is by confessing with your mouth that you are saved. As the Scriptures tell us, "Anyone who believes in him will never be disgraced."

ROMANS 10:9–11 NLT

The word that saves is right here, as near as the tongue in your mouth, as close as the heart in your chest. It's the word of faith that welcomes God to go to work and set things right for us.

ROMANS 10:8 THE MESSAGE

To all who believed him and accepted him, he gave the right to become children of God. They are reborn—not with a physical birth resulting from human passion or plan, but a birth that comes from God.

JOHN 1:12–13 NLT

Therefore, if anyone is in Christ, he is a new creation; old things have passed away; behold, all things have become new.

2 CORINTHIANS 5:17 NKJV

God our Savior showed us how good and kind he is. He saved us because of his mercy, and not because of any good things that we have done. God washed us by the power of the Holy Spirit. He gave us new birth and a fresh beginning. God sent Jesus Christ our Savior to give us his Spirit. Jesus treated us much better than we deserve. He made us acceptable to God and gave us the hope of eternal life.

TITUS 3:4–7 CEV

If we say we have fellowship with God, but we continue living in darkness, we are liars and do not follow the truth. But if we live in the light, as God is in the light, we can share fellowship with each other. Then the blood of Jesus, God's Son, cleanses us from every sin. If we say we have no sin, we are fooling ourselves, and the truth is not in us. But if we confess our sins,

he will forgive our sins, because we can trust God to do
what is right. He will cleanse us from all the wrongs we
have done.

1 JOHN 1:6–9 NCV

— PRAYER —

Say the welcoming word to God—"Jesus is my
Master"—embracing, body and soul, God's work of
doing in us what he did in raising Jesus from the dead.
That's it. You're not "doing" anything; you're simply
calling out to God, trusting him to do it for you. That's
salvation. With your whole being you embrace God
setting things right, and then you say it, right out loud:
"God has set everything right between him and me!"

ROMANS 10:9–10 THE MESSAGE

God, the Bible calls you
our Father in heaven.
How are you like
a father to me?

He surrounds me with loving-kindness and tender mer-
cies. He fills my life with good things!

PSALM 103:4–5 TLB

The Lord is compassionate and merciful; slow to get
angry and filled with unfailing love. He will not constantly accuse us, nor remain angry forever. He does not
punish us for all our sins; he does not deal harshly with
us, as we deserve. For his unfailing love toward those
who fear him is as great as the height of the heavens
above the earth. He has removed our sins as far from us
as the east is from the west.

The Lord is like a father to his children, tender and
compassionate to those who fear him. For he knows how
weak we are; he remembers we are only dust.

PSALM 103:8–14 NLT

Whatever is good and perfect comes down to us from
God our Father, who created all the lights in the heavens. He never changes or casts a shifting shadow.

He chose to give birth to us by giving us his true word. And we, out of all creation, became his prized possession.

JAMES 1:17–18 NLT

If God gives such attention to the appearance of wild-flowers—most of which are never even seen—don't you think he'll attend to you, take pride in you, do his best for you?

MATTHEW 6:30 THE MESSAGE

I will instruct you and teach you in the way which you should go; I will counsel you with My eye upon you.

PSALM 32:8 NASB

Your ears shall hear a word behind you, saying, "This is the way, walk in it," whenever you turn to the right hand or whenever you turn to the left.

ISAIAH 30:21 NKJV

The Lord corrects the people he loves and disciplines those he calls his own.

HEBREWS 12:6 CEV

The Father is a merciful God, who always gives us comfort. He comforts us when we are in trouble, so that we can share that same comfort with others in trouble.

2 CORINTHIANS 1:3–4 CEV

And we have known and believed the love that God has for us. God is love. . . . We love Him because He first loved us.

1 JOHN 4:16, 19 NKJV

We used to be stupid, disobedient, and foolish, as well as slaves of all sorts of desires and pleasures. We were evil and jealous. Everyone hated us, and we hated everyone. God our Savior showed us how good and kind he is. He saved us because of his mercy, and not because of any good things that we have done. God washed us by the power of the Holy Spirit. He gave us new birth and a fresh beginning. God sent Jesus Christ our Savior to give us his Spirit.

TITUS 3:3–6 CEV

It was all his doing; we had nothing to do with it. He gave us a good bath, and we came out of it new people, washed inside and out by the Holy Spirit.

TITUS 3:4–7 THE MESSAGE

— PROMISES —

For the eyes of the Lord run to and fro throughout the whole earth, to show Himself strong on behalf of those whose heart is loyal to Him.

2 CHRONICLES 16:9 NKJV

He is a rewarder of those who diligently seek Him.

HEBREWS 11:6 NKJV

The Lord is faithful, and He will strengthen and protect you from the evil one.

2 Thessalonians 3:3 NASB

As a mother comforts her child, so will I comfort you.

Isaiah 66:13 NIV

And therefore the Lord [earnestly] waits [expecting, looking, and longing] to be gracious to you; and therefore He lifts Himself up, that He may have mercy on you and show loving-kindness to you. . . . Blessed (happy, fortunate, to be envied) are all those who [earnestly] wait for Him, who expect and look and long for Him [for His victory, His favor, His love, His peace, His joy, and His matchless, unbroken companionship]! . . . He will surely be gracious to you at the sound of your cry; when He hears it, He will answer you.

Isaiah 30:18–19 AMP

Can a mother forget the baby at her breast and have no compassion on the child she has borne? Though she may forget, I will not forget you! See, I have engraved you on the palms of my hands.

Isaiah 49:15–16 NIV

"They will be mine," says the Lord Almighty, "in the day when I make up my treasured possession. I will spare them, just as in compassion a man spares his son who serves him."

Malachi 3:17 NIV

The Lord your God in your midst, The Mighty One, will save; He will rejoice over you with gladness, He will quiet you with His love, He will rejoice over you with singing.

ZEPHANIAH 3:17 NKJV

The Lord is gracious and compassionate, slow to anger and rich in love. The Lord is good to all; he has compassion on all he has made.

PSALM 145:8–9 NIV

I know about God the Father and have received Jesus as my Savior. What is the Holy Spirit's role in my life?

I will give you a new heart and put a new spirit in you; I will remove from you your heart of stone and give you a heart of flesh. And I will put my Spirit in you and move you to follow my decrees and be careful to keep my laws.

EZEKIEL 36:26–27 NIV

— INSTRUCTIONS —

He washed away our sins, giving us a new birth and new life through the Holy Spirit. He generously poured out the Spirit upon us through Jesus Christ our Savior.

TITUS 3:5–6 NLT

The name of our Lord Jesus Christ and the power of God's Spirit have washed you and made you holy and acceptable to God.

1 CORINTHIANS 6:11 CEV

The power of the life-giving Spirit has freed you from the power of sin that leads to death.

ROMANS 8:2 NLT

You received God's Spirit when he adopted you as his own children. Now we call him, "Abba, Father." For his Spirit joins our spirit to affirm that we are God's children. And since we are his children, we are his heirs. In fact, together with Christ we are heirs of God's glory. But if we are to share his glory, we must also share his suffering.

ROMANS 8:15–17 NLT

The Holy Spirit produces this kind of fruit in our lives: love, joy, peace, patience, kindness, goodness, faithfulness, gentleness, and self-control.

GALATIANS 5:22–23 NLT

The Friend, the Holy Spirit whom the Father will send at my request, will make everything plain to you. He will remind you of all the things I have told you.

JOHN 14:26 THE MESSAGE

Jesus said to his disciples: If you love me, you will do as I command. Then I will ask the Father to send you the Holy Spirit who will help you and always be with you. The Spirit will show you what is true. The people of this world cannot accept the Spirit, because they don't see or know him. But you know the Spirit, who is with you and will keep on living in you.

JOHN 14:15–17 CEV

The Spirit shows what is true and will come and guide you into the full truth. The Spirit doesn't speak on his own. He will tell you only what he has heard from me, and he will let you know what is going to happen.

JOHN 16:13 CEV

When the Comforter (Counselor, Helper, Advocate, Intercessor, Strengthener, Standby) comes, whom I will send to you from the Father, the Spirit of Truth who comes (proceeds) from the Father, He [Himself] will testify regarding Me.

JOHN 15:26 AMP

As it is written in the Scriptures: "No one has ever seen this, and no one has ever heard about it. No one has ever imagined what God has prepared for those who love him." But God has shown us these things through the Spirit.

The Spirit searches out all things, even the deep secrets of God. Who knows the thoughts that another person has? Only a person's spirit that lives within him knows his thoughts. It is the same with God. No one knows the thoughts of God except the Spirit of God. Now we did not receive the spirit of the world, but we received the Spirit that is from God so that we can know all that God has given us.

1 CORINTHIANS 2:9–12 NCV

Those who trust God's action in them find that God's Spirit is in them—living and breathing God!

ROMANS 8:5 THE MESSAGE

The Holy Spirit helps us in our weakness. For example, we don't know what God wants us to pray for. But the Holy Spirit prays for us with groanings that cannot be expressed in words. And the Father who knows all hearts knows what the Spirit is saying, for the Spirit pleads for us believers in harmony with God's own will.

ROMANS 8:26–27 NLT

Dear friends, use your most holy faith to build yourselves up, praying in the Holy Spirit.

JUDE 20 NCV

Pray in the Spirit at all times with all kinds of prayers, asking for everything you need.

EPHESIANS 6:18 NCV

On the final and climactic day of the Feast, Jesus took his stand. He cried out, "If anyone thirsts, let him come to me and drink. Rivers of living water will brim and spill out of the depths of anyone who believes in me this way, just as the Scripture says." (He said this in regard to the Spirit, whom those who believed in him were about to receive. The Spirit had not yet been given because Jesus had not yet been glorified.)

JOHN 7:37–39 THE MESSAGE

He gave them this command: "Do not leave Jerusalem, but wait for the gift my Father promised, which you have heard me speak about. For John baptized with water, but in a few days you will be baptized with the Holy Spirit."

ACTS 1:4–5 NIV

You will receive power when the Holy Spirit comes on you; and you will be my witnesses in Jerusalem, and in all Judea and Samaria, and to the ends of the earth.

ACTS 1:8 NIV

And everyone present was filled with the Holy Spirit and began speaking in languages they didn't know, for the Holy Spirit gave them this ability.

ACTS 2:4 TLB

Then Peter stepped forward with the eleven other apostles and shouted to the crowd. . . . "What you see was predicted long ago by the prophet Joel: 'In the last days,' God says, 'I will pour out my Spirit upon all people. Your sons and daughters will prophesy. Your young men will see visions, and your old men will dream dreams. In those days I will pour out my Spirit even on my servants—men and women alike—and they will prophesy.'"

ACTS 2:14, 16–18 NLT

Jesus was lifted up to heaven and is now at God's right side. The Father has given the Holy Spirit to Jesus as he promised. So Jesus has poured out that Spirit, and this is what you now see and hear.

ACTS 2:33 NCV

Peter said to them, "Change your hearts and lives and be baptized, each one of you, in the name of Jesus Christ for the forgiveness of your sins. And you will receive the gift of the Holy Spirit. This promise is for you, for your children, and for all who are far away. It is for everyone the Lord our God calls to himself."

ACTS 2:38–39 NCV

While Peter was still speaking these words, the Holy Spirit came on all who heard the message. The circumcised believers who had come with Peter were astonished that the gift of the Holy Spirit had been poured out even on the Gentiles. For they heard them speaking in tongues and praising God. Then Peter said, "Can anyone keep these people from being baptized with water? They have received the Holy Spirit just as we have."

ACTS 10:44–47 NIV

When Paul placed his hands on them, the Holy Spirit came on them, and they spoke in tongues and prophesied.

ACTS 19:6 NIV

Don't be drunk with wine, because that will ruin your life. Instead, be filled with the Holy Spirit, singing psalms and hymns and spiritual songs among yourselves, and making music to the Lord in your hearts. And give thanks for everything to God the Father in the name of our Lord Jesus Christ.

EPHESIANS 5:18–20 NLT

How can I please you, God?

Then one of the scribes . . . asked Him, "Which is the first commandment of all?" Jesus answered him, "The first of all the commandments is: 'Hear, O Israel, the Lord our God, the Lord is one. And you shall love the Lord your God with all your heart, with all your soul, with all your mind, and with all your strength.' This is the first commandment. And the second, like it, is this: 'You shall love your neighbor as yourself.' There is no other commandment greater than these."

MARK 12:28–31 NKJV

The Lord delights in those who fear him, who put their hope in his unfailing love.

PSALM 147:11 NIV

God is Spirit, and those who worship Him must worship in spirit and truth.

JOHN 4:24 NKJV

That's the kind of people the Father is out looking for: those who are simply and honestly themselves before him in their worship. . . . Those who worship him must do it out of their very being, their spirits, their true selves, in adoration.

JOHN 4:23–24 THE MESSAGE

— INSTRUCTIONS —

Give unto the Lord the glory due to His name; worship the Lord in the beauty of holiness.

PSALM 29:2 NKJV

Rejoice always, pray without ceasing, in everything give thanks; for this is the will of God in Christ Jesus for you.

1 THESSALONIANS 5:16–18 NKJV

Sing, sing your hearts out to God! Let every detail in your lives—words, actions, whatever—be done in the name of the Master, Jesus, thanking God the Father every step of the way.

COLOSSIANS 3:17 THE MESSAGE

Celebrate God all day, every day. I mean, revel in him! . . . Don't fret or worry. Instead of worrying, pray. Let petitions and praises shape your worries into prayers, letting God know your concerns. Before you know it, a sense of God's wholeness, everything coming together for good, will come and settle you down. It's wonderful what happens when Christ displaces worry at the center of your life.

PHILIPPIANS 4:4, 6–7 THE MESSAGE

Trust in Him at all times, O people; pour out your heart before Him; God is a refuge for us.

PSALM 62:8 NASB

Fix these words of mine in your hearts and minds. . . . Teach them to your children, talking about them when you sit at home and when you walk along the road, when you lie down and when you get up.

DEUTERONOMY 11:18–19 NIV

Every part of Scripture is God-breathed and useful one way or another—showing us truth, exposing our rebellion, correcting our mistakes, training us to live God's way.

2 TIMOTHY 3:16 THE MESSAGE

— PRAYERS —

May God, who puts all things together, makes all things whole. . . . Now put you together, provide you with everything you need to please him, make us into what gives him most pleasure, by means of the sacrifice of Jesus, the Messiah.

HEBREWS 13:20–21 THE MESSAGE

May the words of my mouth and the meditation of my heart be pleasing in your sight, O Lord, my Rock and my Redeemer.

PSALM 19:14 NIV

— EXAMPLE —

*David was a man who pleased the Lord. In fact, the
Bible gives him this commendation:*

I've searched the land and found this David, son of
Jesse. He's a man whose heart beats to my heart, a man
who will do what I tell him.

ACTS 13:22 THE MESSAGE

What was David's secret? He understood and enjoyed
the grace of God. He had a deep love and respect for
the Lord and a great desire to express that love in worship: God—you're my God! I can't get enough of you!
I've worked up such hunger and thirst for God, traveling
across dry and weary deserts. So here I am in the place of
worship, eyes open, drinking in your strength and glory.
In your generous love I am really living at last! My lips
brim praises like fountains. I bless you every time I take
a breath; my arms wave like banners of praise to you.

PSALM 63:1–4 THE MESSAGE

Thank you! Everything in me says "Thank you!" Angels
listen as I sing my thanks. I kneel in worship facing your
holy temple and say it again: "Thank you!" Thank you
for your love, thank you for your faithfulness.

PSALM 138:1–2 THE MESSAGE

I just blew it again, Lord. Am I still saved?

In the past all of us lived like them, trying to please our sinful selves and doing all the things our bodies and minds wanted. We should have suffered God's anger because of the way we were. . . . But God's mercy is great, and he loved us very much. Though we were spiritually dead because of the things we did against God, he gave us new life with Christ. You have been saved by God's grace.

EPHESIANS 2:3–5 NCV

— INSTRUCTIONS —

You have been saved by grace through believing. You did not save yourselves; it was a gift from God. It was not the result of your own efforts, so you cannot brag about it.

EPHESIANS 2:8–9 NCV

Clearly, God's promise to give the whole earth to Abraham and his descendants was based not on his obedience to God's law, but on a right relationship with God that comes by faith. If God's promise is only for those who obey the law, then faith is not necessary and the promise is pointless. So the promise is received by faith.

It is given as a free gift. And we are all certain to receive it . . . if we have faith like Abraham's.

ROMANS 4:13–14, 16 NLT

Can't you see the central issue in all this? It is not what you and I do. . . . It is what God is doing, and he is creating something totally new, a free life!

GALATIANS 6:15 THE MESSAGE

— PROMISES —

The fulfillment of God's promise depends entirely on trusting God and his way, and then simply embracing him and what he does. God's promise arrives as pure gift. That's the only way everyone can be sure to get in on it.

ROMANS 4:16 THE MESSAGE

God has given us eternal life, and this life is in His Son. He who has the Son has life; he who does not have the Son of God does not have life. These things I have written to you who believe in the name of the Son of God, that you may know that you have eternal life, and that you may continue to believe in the name of the Son of God.

1 JOHN 5:11–13 NKJV

Yet to all who received him, to those who believed in his name, he gave the right to become children of God.

JOHN 1:12 NIV

I tell you the truth, whoever hears what I say and believes in the One who sent me has eternal life. That person will not be judged guilty but has already left death and entered life.

JOHN 5:24 NCV

My sheep hear My voice, and I know them, and they follow Me; and I give eternal life to them, and they will never perish; and no one will snatch them out of My hand.

JOHN 10:27–28 NASB

For it is God Who is all the while effectually at work in you [energizing and creating in you the power and desire], both to will and to work for His good pleasure and satisfaction and delight.

PHILIPPIANS 2:13 AMP

I will lead the blind by ways they have not known . . . I will turn the darkness into light before them and make the rough places smooth. These are the things I will do; I will not forsake them.

ISAIAH 42:16 NIV

By entering through faith into what God has always wanted to do for us—set us right with him, make us fit for him—we have it all together with God because of our Master Jesus. And that's not all: We throw open our doors to God and discover at the same moment that he has already thrown open his door to us. We find ourselves standing where we always hoped we might stand—out in the wide open spaces of God's grace and glory, standing tall and shouting our praise.

ROMANS 5:1–3 THE MESSAGE

And you shall know [with an acquaintance and understanding based on and grounded in personal experience] that I am the Lord; for they shall not be put to shame who wait for, look for, hope for, and expect Me. . . . For thus says the Lord: Even the captives of the mighty shall be taken away, and the prey of the terrible shall be delivered; for I will contend with him who contends with you.

ISAIAH 49:23–25 AMP

For He Himself has said, "I will never leave you nor forsake you."

HEBREWS 13:5 NKJV

— PRAYER —

I pray for you constantly, asking God, the glorious Father of our Lord Jesus Christ, to give you wisdom to see clearly and really understand who Christ is and all that he has done for you. I pray that your hearts will be flooded with light so that you can see something of the future he has called you to share. . . . I pray that you will begin to understand how incredibly great his power is to help those who believe him. It is that same mighty power that raised Christ from the dead and seated him in the place of honor at God's right hand in heaven.

EPHESIANS 1:16–20 TLB

— EXAMPLES —

Abraham received right standing with God by faith, apart from any good works that he did. The Bible calls him the "father of all people who embrace what God does for them."

ROMANS 4:11 THE MESSAGE

When everything was hopeless, Abraham believed anyway, deciding to live not on the basis of what he saw he couldn't do but on what God said he would do. . . . He didn't tiptoe around God's promise asking cautiously skeptical questions. He plunged into the promise and came up strong, ready for God, sure that God would make good on what he had said. That's why it is said, "Abraham was declared fit before God by trusting God to set him right."

ROMANS 4:17, 20–22 THE MESSAGE

And when God counted him as righteous, it wasn't just for Abraham's benefit. It was recorded for our benefit, too, assuring us that God will also count us as righteous if we believe in him, the one who raised Jesus our Lord from the dead. He was handed over to die because of our sins, and he was raised to life to make us right with God.

ROMANS 4:23–25 NLT

What about prayer?
Is there a certain way
I should pray?

This is what I want you to do: Ask the Father for whatever is in keeping with the things I've revealed to you. Ask in my name, according to my will, and he'll most certainly give it to you.

JOHN 16:23–24 THE MESSAGE

— INSTRUCTIONS —

Keep on asking, and you will receive what you ask for. Keep on seeking, and you will find. Keep on knocking, and the door will be opened to you. For everyone who asks, receives. Everyone who seeks, finds. And to everyone who knocks, the door will be opened. You parents—if your children ask for a loaf of bread, do you give them a stone instead? Or if they ask for a fish, do you give them a snake? Of course not! So if you sinful people know how to give good gifts to your children, how much more will your heavenly Father give good gifts to those who ask him.

MATTHEW 7:7–11 NLT

I am the vine, and you are the branches. If you stay joined to me, and I stay joined to you, then you will produce lots of fruit. But you cannot do anything without me. Stay joined to me and let my teachings become part of you. Then you can pray for whatever you want, and your prayer will be answered.

JOHN 15:5–7 CEV

God is strong, and he wants you strong. So take everything the Master has set out for you, well-made weapons of the best materials. And put them to use so you will be able to stand up to everything the Devil throws your way. This is no afternoon athletic contest that we'll walk away from and forget about in a couple of hours. This is for keeps, a life-or-death fight to the finish against the Devil and all his angels.

Be prepared. You're up against far more than you can handle on your own. Take all the help you can get, every weapon God has issued, so that when it's all over but the shouting you'll still be on your feet. . . . God's Word is an indispensable weapon. In the same way, prayer is essential in this ongoing warfare. Pray hard and long.

EPHESIANS 6:10–18 THE MESSAGE

Never give up praying. And when you pray, keep alert and be thankful.

COLOSSIANS 4:2 CEV

Always pray by the power of the Spirit.

EPHESIANS 6:18 CEV

I will pray with the spirit, and I will also pray with the understanding.

1 CORINTHIANS 14:15 NKJV

— PROMISES —

The Lord is near to all who call upon Him, to all who call upon Him in truth. He will fulfill the desire of those who fear Him; He will also hear their cry and will save them.

PSALM 145:18–19 NASB

The eyes of the Lord are on the righteous, and His ears are open to their cry. . . . The righteous cry out, and the Lord hears, and delivers them out of all their troubles.

PSALM 34:15, 17 NKJV

Before they call, I will answer; and while they are still speaking, I will hear.

ISAIAH 65:24 NKJV

Then said the Lord to me . . . "I am alert and active, watching over My word to perform it."

JEREMIAH 1:12 AMP

This is the confidence which we have before Him, that, if we ask anything according to His will, He hears us. And if we know that He hears us in whatever we ask, we know that we have the requests which we have asked from Him.

1 JOHN 5:14–15 NASB

[Jesus said,] "Again, I tell you that if two of you on earth agree about anything you ask for, it will be done for you by my Father in heaven. For where two or three come together in my name, there am I with them."

MATTHEW 18:19–20 NIV

And Jesus, replying, said to them, "Have faith in God [constantly]. Truly, I tell you, whoever says to this mountain, 'Be lifted up and thrown into the sea!' and does not doubt at all in his heart but believes that what he says will take place, it will be done for him. For this reason I am telling you, whatever you ask for in prayer, believe (trust and be confident) that it is granted to you, and you will [get it]."

MARK 11:22–24 AMP

Let us then fearlessly and confidently and boldly draw near to the throne of grace . . . that we may receive mercy [for our failures] and find grace to help in good time for every need [appropriate help and well-timed help, coming just when we need it].

HEBREWS 4:16 AMP

The earnest (heartfelt, continued) prayer of a righteous man makes tremendous power available [dynamic in its working].

JAMES 5:16 AMP

With God's power working in us, God can do much, much more than anything we can ask or imagine.

EPHESIANS 3:20 NCV

— PRAYERS —

I pray that Christ will live in your hearts by faith and
that your life will be strong in love and be built on love.
And I pray that you . . . will have the power to understand the greatness of Christ's love—how wide and how
long and how high and how deep that love is. Christ's
love is greater than anyone can ever know, but I pray
that you will be able to know that love. Then you can be
filled with the fullness of God.

EPHESIANS 3:17–19 NCV

We ask God to give you complete knowledge of his will
and to give you spiritual wisdom and understanding.
Then the way you live will always honor and please the
Lord, and your lives will produce every of good fruit.
All the while, you will grow as you learn to know God
better and better. We also pray that you will be strengthened with all his glorious power so you will have all
the endurance and patience you need. May you be filled
with joy, always thanking the Father.

COLOSSIANS 1:9–12 NLT

I NEED SOME ADVICE. CAN YOU HELP ME?

Lord, I face so many decisions daily. Where can I turn for direction and guidance?

If you need wisdom, ask our generous God, and he will give it to you. He will not rebuke you for asking.

JAMES 1:5 NLT

— INSTRUCTIONS —

Call to me and I will answer you and tell you great and unsearchable things you do not know.

JEREMIAH 33:3 NIV

My child, listen to what I say and treasure my commands. Tune your ears to wisdom, and concentrate on understanding. . . . Search for them as you would for silver; seek them like hidden treasures. Then you will understand what it means to fear the Lord, and you will gain knowledge of God.

PROVERBS 2:1–2, 4–5 NLT

Trust God from the bottom of your heart. Don't try to figure out everything on your own. Listen for God's voice in everything you do, everywhere you go. He's the one who will keep you on track. Don't assume that you know it all. Run to God!

PROVERBS 3:5–7 THE MESSAGE

All Scripture is inspired by God and is useful to teach us what is true and to make us realize what is wrong in our lives. It corrects us when we are wrong and teaches us to do what is right. God uses it to prepare and equip his people to do every good work.

2 TIMOTHY 3:16–17 NLT

— PROMISES —

I will instruct you and teach you in the way you should go; I will counsel you and watch over you.

PSALM 32:8 NIV

Your word is a lamp to my feet and a light to my path.

PSALM 119:105 NKJV

The statutes of the Lord are trustworthy, making wise the simple. The precepts of the Lord are right, giving joy to the heart. The commands of the Lord are radiant, giving light to the eyes. . . . By them is your servant warned; in keeping them there is great reward.

PSALM 19:7–8, 11 NIV

— PRAYERS —

Send forth your light and your truth, let them guide me.

PSALM 43:3 NIV

Show me the path, O Lord; point out the road for me to follow. Lead me by your truth and teach me, for you are the God who saves me. All day long I put my hope in you.
    PSALM 25:4–5 NLT

Teach me to do your will, for you are my God. May your gracious Spirit lead me forward on a firm footing.
    PSALM 143:10 NLT

Give me an understanding mind so that I can govern your people well and know the difference between what is right and what is wrong. For who by himself is able to carry such a heavy responsibility?
    1 KINGS 3:9 TLB

Your statutes are my delight; they are my counselors.
    PSALM 119:24 NIV

— EXAMPLE —

When an enemy army came against Jehoshaphat, he sought the Lord for wisdom and guidance:

"We have no power to face this vast army that is attacking us. We do not know what to do, but our eyes are upon you.". . . Then the Spirit of the Lord came upon Jahaziel. . . . He said . . . "This is what the Lord says to you: 'Do not be afraid or discouraged because of this vast army. For the battle is not yours, but God's. . . Go out to face them tomorrow, and the Lord will be with you.' "
    2 CHRONICLES 20:12, 14–15, 17 NIV

Lord, I can't stop worrying. Is there a way to find peace of mind?

Don't fret or worry. Instead of worrying, pray. Let petitions and praises shape your worries into prayers, letting God know your concerns. Before you know it, a sense of God's wholeness, everything coming together for good, will come and settle you down. It's wonderful what happens when Christ displaces worry at the center of your life.

PHILIPPIANS 4:6–8 THE MESSAGE

— INSTRUCTIONS —

Cast your burden on the Lord, and He shall sustain you; He shall never permit the righteous to be moved.

PSALM 55:22 NKJV

[Cast] the whole of your care [all your anxieties, all your worries, all your concerns, once and for all] on Him, for He cares for you affectionately and cares about you watchfully.

1 PETER 5:7 AMP

— PROMISES —

I am leaving you with a gift—peace of mind and heart.
And the peace I give is a gift the world cannot give. So
don't be troubled or afraid.

JOHN 14:27 NLT

The Lord is my Light and my Salvation—whom shall I
fear or dread? The Lord is the Refuge and Stronghold of
my life—of whom shall I be afraid?

PSALM 27:1 AMP

In righteousness you shall be established; you shall be
far from oppression, for you shall not fear; and from terror, for it shall not come near you.

ISAIAH 54:14 NKJV

Those who live in the shelter of the Most High will find
rest in the shadow of the Almighty. This I declare about
the Lord: He alone is my refuge, my place of safety; he
is my God, and I trust him.

PSALM 91:1–2 NLT

You are my hiding place; you will protect me from trouble and surround me with songs of deliverance.

PSALM 32:7 NIV

For he will rescue you from every trap and protect
you from deadly disease. He will cover you with his
feathers. He will shelter you with his wings. His faithful promises are your armor and protection. Do not be

afraid of the terrors of the night, nor arrow that flies in the day. . . . Though a thousand fall at your side, though ten thousand are dying around you, these evils will not touch you. . . . For he will order his angels to protect you wherever you go.

PSALM 91:3–5, 7, 11 NLT

The Lord says, "I will rescue those who love me. I will protect those who trust in my name. When they call on me, I will answer; I will be with them in trouble. I will rescue them and honor them. I will reward them with a long life and give them my salvation."

PSALM 91:14–16 NLT

But the Lord is faithful, and he will strengthen and protect you from the evil one.

2 THESSALONIANS 3:3 NIV

The angel of the Lord encamps around those who fear Him, and rescues them.

PSALM 34:7 NASB

— PRAYERS —

May the God of hope fill you with all joy and peace as you trust in him, so that you may overflow with hope by the power of the Holy Spirit.

ROMANS 15:13 NIV

In the multitude of my [anxious] thoughts within me, Your comforts cheer and delight my soul!

PSALM 94:19 AMP

— EXAMPLE —

During the night of the first Passover, God protected His people. As they trusted and obeyed Him, they were kept safe:

Then Moses summoned all the elders of Israel and said to them, "Go at once and . . . slaughter the Passover lamb. Take a bunch of hyssop, dip it into the blood in the basin and put some of the blood on the top and on both sides of the doorframe. Not one of you shall go out the door of his house until morning. When the Lord goes through the land . . . he will see the blood . . . and will pass over that doorway, and he will not permit the destroyer to enter your houses and strike you down."

EXODUS 12:21–23 NIV

I want my life to count. How can I reach my full potential?

It's not possible for a person to succeed—I'm talking about eternal success—without heaven's help.

JOHN 3:27 THE MESSAGE

Unless the Lord builds the house, they labor in vain who build it; unless the Lord guards the city, the watchman keeps awake in vain.

PSALM 127:1 NASB

O Lord my God . . . Your plans for us are too numerous to list. . . . If I tried to recite all your wonderful deeds, I would never come to the end of them.

PSALM 40:5 NLT

— INSTRUCTIONS —

In his heart a man plans his course, but the Lord determines his steps.

PROVERBS 16:9 NIV

We humans keep brainstorming options and plans, but God's purpose prevails.

PROVERBS 19:21 THE MESSAGE

You're blessed when you stay on course, walking steadily on the road revealed by God. You're blessed when you follow his directions, doing your best to find him. That's right—you don't go off on your own; you walk straight along the road he set.

PSALM 119:1–3 THE MESSAGE

Devote yourselves to prayer with an alert mind and a thankful heart.

COLOSSIANS 4:2 NLT

This book of the law [the Word of God] shall not depart from your mouth, but you shall meditate on it day and night, so that you may be careful to do according to all that is written in it; for then you will make your way prosperous, and then you will have success.

JOSHUA 1:8 NASB

Be strong and do not give up, for your work will be rewarded.

2 CHRONICLES 15:7 NIV

No matter how much you want, laziness won't help a bit, but hard work will reward you with more than enough.

PROVERBS 13:4 CEV

Refuse good advice and watch your plans fail; take good counsel and watch them succeed.

PROVERBS 15:22 THE MESSAGE

Form your purpose by asking for counsel, then carry it out using all the help you can get.

PROVERBS 20:18 THE MESSAGE

If you do your job well, you will work for a ruler and never be a slave.

PROVERBS 22:29 CEV

A lazy life is an empty life.

PROVERBS 12:27 THE MESSAGE

Whoever wants to be great must become a servant.

MATTHEW 20:26 THE MESSAGE

— PROMISES —

"For I know the plans I have for you," declares the Lord, "plans to prosper you and not to harm you, plans to give you hope and a future. Then you will call upon me and come and pray to me, and I will listen to you. You will seek me and find me when you seek me with all your heart."

JEREMIAH 29:11–13 NIV

God can pour on the blessings in astonishing ways so that you're ready for anything and everything.

2 CORINTHIANS 9:8 THE MESSAGE

I can do all things through Christ, because he gives me strength.

PHILIPPIANS 4:13 NCV

We are God's workmanship, created in Christ Jesus to do good works, which God prepared in advance for us to do.

EPHESIANS 2:10 NIV

— PRAYERS —

I pray for good fortune in everything you do, and for your good health—that your everyday affairs prosper, as well as your soul!

3 JOHN 2 THE MESSAGE

We pray for God's power to help you do all the good things that you hope to do and that your faith makes you want to do. Then . . . you will bring honor to the name of our Lord Jesus, and he will bring honor to you.

2 THESSALONIANS 1:11–12 CEV

May the God of peace . . . equip you with all you need for doing his will. May he produce in you, through the power of Jesus Christ, every good thing that is pleasing to him.

HEBREWS 13:20–21 NLT

— EXAMPLE —

God chose Solomon to build the temple in Jerusalem. His father, King David, encouraged him again and again, reminding him that the Lord would be with him as he worked to fulfill God's plan for his life:

David also said to Solomon his son, "Be strong and courageous, and do the work. Do not be afraid or discouraged, for the Lord God, my God, is with you. He will not fail you or forsake you until all the work for the service of the temple of theLord is finished."

1 CHRONICLES 28:20 NIV

Nothing is going right! Is there a way to keep my joy no matter what happens?

You are my hiding place! You protect me from trouble, and you put songs in my heart.

PSALM 32:7 CEV

I was pushed back and about to fall, but the Lord helped me. The Lord is my strength and my song; he has become my salvation.

PSALM 118:13–14 NIV

— INSTRUCTIONS —

Let all who take refuge in you be glad; let them ever sing for joy. Spread your protection over them, that those who love your name may rejoice in you. For surely, O Lord, you bless the righteous; you surround them with your favor as with a shield.

PSALM 5:11–12 NIV

Let the godly rejoice. Let them be glad in God's presence. Let them be filled with joy. Sing praises to God and to his name! Sing loud praises to him who rides the clouds. His name is the Lord—rejoice in his presence!

PSALM 68:3–4 NLT

Let the heavens rejoice, and let the earth be glad; and let them say among the nations, "The Lord reigns." . . . Oh, give thanks to the Lord, for He is good! For His mercy endures forever.

1 CHRONICLES 16:31, 34 NKJV

Celebrate God all day, every day. I mean, revel in him!

PHILIPPIANS 4:4 THE MESSAGE

Speak to each other with psalms, hymns, and spiritual songs, singing and making music in your hearts to the Lord. Always give thanks to God the Father for everything, in the name of our Lord Jesus Christ.

EPHESIANS 5:19–20 NCV

And you shall rejoice before the Lord your God in all that you undertake.

DEUTERONOMY 12:18 AMP

Do everything without complaining.

PHILIPPIANS 2:14 NCV

Dear brothers and sisters, when troubles come your way, consider it an opportunity for great joy. For you know that when your faith is tested, your endurance has a chance to grow. So let it grow, for when your endurance is fully developed, you will be perfect and complete, needing nothing.

JAMES 1:2–4 NLT

Though you have not seen him, you love him; and even though you do not see him now, you believe in him and are filled with an inexpressible and glorious joy.

1 PETER 1:8 NIV

— PRAYERS —

I will sing to the Lord as long as I live; I will sing praise to my God while I have my being. May my meditation be sweet to Him; I will be glad in the Lord.

PSALM 104:33–34 NKJV

I will greatly rejoice in the Lord, my soul shall be joyful in my God; for He has clothed me with the garments of salvation, He has covered me with the robe of righteousness . . . as a bride adorns herself with her jewels.

ISAIAH 61:10 NKJV

It is good to say thank you to the Lord, to sing praises to the God who is above all gods. Every morning tell him, "Thank you for your kindness," and every evening rejoice in all his faithfulness. . . . You have done so much for me, O Lord. No wonder I am glad! I sing for joy.

PSALM 92:1–2, 4 TLB

Why are you cast down, O my inner self? And why should you moan over me and be disquieted within me? Hope in God and wait expectantly for Him, for I shall yet praise Him, Who is the help of my [sad] countenance, and my God.

PSALM 43:5 AMP

— PROMISES —

Though a righteous man falls seven times, he rises again.
PROVERBS 24:16 NIV

Blessed (happy, to be envied) is the man who is patient
under trial and stands up under temptation, for when he
has stood the test and been approved, he will receive
[the victor's] crown of life which God has promised to
those who love Him.
JAMES 1:12 AMP

We also have joy with our troubles, because we know
that these troubles produce patience. And patience produces character, and character produces hope. And this
hope will never disappoint us, because God has poured
out his love to fill our hearts.
ROMANS 5:3–5 NCV

— EXAMPLE —

Just after God warns him of an impending invasion,
Habakkuk declares that his joy is not based on his cir-
cumstances but in his God:

Fig trees may no longer bloom, or vineyards produce
grapes; olive trees may be fruitless, and harvest time a failure; sheep pens may be empty, and cattle stalls
vacant—but I will still celebrate because the
Lord God saves me. The Lord gives me
my strength.
HABAKKUK 3:17–19 CEV

I have made a terrible mistake and I feel so guilty. What should I do?

I'm glad . . . that you were jarred into turning things around. You let the distress bring you to God, not drive you from him. The result was all gain, no loss. Distress that drives us to God does that. It turns us around. It gets us back in the way of salvation. We never regret that kind of pain. But those who let distress drive them away from God are full of regrets, end up on a deathbed of regrets.

And now, isn't it wonderful all the ways in which this distress has goaded you closer to God? You're more alive, more concerned, more sensitive, more reverent, more human, more passionate, more responsible. Looked at from any angle, you've come out of this with purity of heart.

2 CORINTHIANS 7:9–11 THE MESSAGE

Just see what this godly sorrow produced in you! . . . You showed that you have done everything necessary to make things right.

2 CORINTHIANS 7:11 NLT

— INSTRUCTIONS —

He who conceals his sins does not prosper, but whoever confesses and renounces them finds mercy.

PROVERBS 28:13 NIV

Blessed is he whose transgressions are forgiven, whose sins are covered. Blessed is the man whose sin the Lord does not count against him.

PSALM 32:1–2 NIV

When I kept it all inside, my bones turned to powder, my words became daylong groans. The pressure never let up; all the juices of my life dried up. Then I let it all out; I said, "I'll make a clean breast of my failures to God." Suddenly the pressure was gone—my guilt dissolved, my sin disappeared.

PSALM 32:3–5 THE MESSAGE

Confess your sins to each other and pray for each other so that you can live together whole and healed. The prayer of a person living right with God is something powerful to be reckoned with.

JAMES 5:16 THE MESSAGE

Now then go, and I, even I, will be with your mouth, and teach you what you are to say.

EXODUS 4:12 NASB

Is anyone crying for help? God is listening, ready to rescue you. If your heart is broken, you'll find God right there.

PSALM 34:17–18 THE MESSAGE

He heals the heartbroken and bandages their wounds.

PSALM 147:3 THE MESSAGE

For thus says the high and lofty One—He Who inhabits eternity, Whose name is Holy: I dwell in the high and holy place, but with him also who is of a thoroughly penitent and humble spirit, to revive the spirit of the humble and to revive the heart of the thoroughly penitent [bruised with sorrow for sin].

ISAIAH 57:15 AMP

If we walk in the Light as He Himself is in the Light, we have fellowship with one another, and the blood of Jesus His Son cleanses us from all sin. If we say that we have no sin, we are deceiving ourselves and the truth is not in us. If we confess our sins, He is faithful and righteous to forgive us our sins and to cleanse us from all unrighteousness.

1 JOHN 1:7–9 NASB

For as high as the heavens are above the earth, so great is his love for those who fear him; as far as the east is from the west, so far has he removed our

transgressions from us. As a father has compassion on his children, so the Lord has compassion on those who fear him.

PSALM 103:11–13 NIV

— PRAYERS —

Create in me a pure heart, O God, and renew a steadfast spirit within me.

PSALM 51:10 NIV

Have mercy on me, O God, according to your unfailing love; according to your great compassion blot out my transgressions. Wash away all my iniquity and cleanse me from my sin. For I know my transgressions, and my sin is always before me.

PSALM 51:1–3 NIV

Now may our Lord Jesus Christ Himself, and our God and Father, who has loved us and given us everlasting consolation and good hope by grace, comfort your hearts and establish you in every good word and work. . . . The Lord is faithful, who will establish you and guard you from the evil one.

2 THESSALONIANS 2:16–17; 3:3 NKJV

— EXAMPLE —

*King David is an example of a man who received God's
forgiveness and then forgave himself:*

I said, "I will confess my transgressions to the Lord,"
and You forgave the iniquity of my sin. . . . You are my
hiding place; You shall preserve me from trouble; You
shall surround me with songs of deliverance. . . . Be glad
in the Lord and rejoice, you righteous; and shout for joy,
all you upright in heart!
    PSALM 32:5, 7, 11 NKJV

*God's gift of righteousness was so real to David that he
was able to once again see himself as one of the righteous,
as one who was upright in heart. And the revelation of
God's mercy made him shout for joy!*

I want to be a good Christian, but I keep messing up. How can I change?

God is working in you, giving you the desire and the power to do what pleases him.

PHILIPPIANS 2:13 NLT

We are God's masterpiece. He has created us anew in Christ Jesus, so we can do the good things he planned for us long ago.

EPHESIANS 2:10 NLT

— INSTRUCTIONS —

Everyone who hears these words of Mine and acts on them, may be compared to a wise man who built his house on the rock. And the rain fell, and the floods came, and the winds blew and slammed against that house; and yet it did not fall, for it had been founded on the rock. Everyone who hears these words of Mine and does not act upon them, will be like a foolish man who built his house on the sand. The rain fell, and the floods came, and the winds blew and slammed against that house; and it fell—and great was its fall.

MATTHEW 7:24–27 NASB

Faith comes by hearing, and hearing by the word of God.

ROMANS 10:17 NKJV

As newborn babes, desire the pure milk of the word, that you may grow thereby.

1 PETER 2:2 NKJV

For you have been born again not of seed which is perishable but imperishable, that is, through the living and enduring word of God.

1 PETER 1:23 NASB

All Scripture is given by God and is useful for teaching, for showing people what is wrong in their lives, for correcting faults, and for teaching how to live right. Using the Scriptures, the person who serves God will be capable, having all that is needed to do every good work.

2 TIMOTHY 3:16–17 NCV

And so, dear brothers and sisters, I plead with you to give your bodies to God because of all he has done for you. Let them be a living and holy sacrifice—the kind he will find acceptable. This is truly the way to worship him. Don't copy the behavior and customs of this world, but let God transform you into a new person by changing the way you think. Then you will learn to know God's will for you, which is good and pleasing and perfect.

ROMANS 12:1–2 NLT

Do not merely listen to the word, and so deceive your-selves. Do what it says. Anyone who listens to the word but does not do what it says is like a man who looks at his face in a mirror and, after looking at himself, goes away and immediately forgets what he looks like. But the man who looks intently into the perfect law that gives freedom, and continues to do this, not forgetting what he has heard, but doing it—he will be blessed in what he does.

JAMES 1:22–25 NIV

This Book of the Law shall not depart from your mouth, but you shall meditate in it day and night, that you may observe to do according to all that is written in it. For then you will make your way prosperous, and then you will have good success.

JOSHUA 1:8 NKJV

— PROMISES —

If any person is [ingrafted] in Christ (the Messiah) he is a new creation (a new creature altogether); the old [pre-vious moral and spiritual condition] has passed away. Behold, the fresh and new has come!

2 CORINTHIANS 5:17 AMP

In the past you were slaves to sin—sin controlled you. But thank God, you fully obeyed the things that you were taught. You were made free from sin, and now you are slaves to goodness.

ROMANS 6:17–18 NCV

And having been set free from sin, you have become the servants of righteousness (of conformity to the divine will in thought, purpose and action).

ROMANS 6:18 AMP

Such is the reliance and confidence that we have through Christ. . . . Not that we are fit (qualified and sufficient in ability) of ourselves . . . but our power and ability and sufficiency are from God. [It is He] Who has qualified us [making us to be fit and worthy and sufficient].

2 CORINTHIANS 3:4–6 AMP

God gives us what it takes to do all that we do.

2 CORINTHIANS 3:5 CEV

— PRAYERS —

We keep on praying for you, that our God . . . will make you as good as you wish you could be!—rewarding your faith with his power. Then everyone will be praising the name of the Lord Jesus Christ because of the results they see in you; and your greatest glory will be that you belong to him. The tender mercy of our God and of the Lord Jesus Christ has made all this possible for you.

2 THESSALONIANS 1:11–12 TLB

We have kept on praying and asking God to help you understand what he wants you to do; asking him to make you wise about spiritual things; and asking that the way you live will always please the Lord and honor him, so that you will always be doing good, kind things for others, while all the time you are learning to know God better and better. We are praying, too, that you will be filled with his mighty, glorious strength so that you can keep going no matter what happens—always full of the joy of the Lord.

COLOSSIANS 1:9–11 TLB

— EXAMPLE —

The apostle Paul experienced a tremendous turnaround in his life after he believed on the Lord Jesus:

Even though I was once a blasphemer and a persecutor and a violent man, I was shown mercy because I acted in ignorance and unbelief. The grace of our Lord was poured out on me abundantly, along with the faith and love that are in Christ Jesus.

1 TIMOTHY 1:13–14 NIV

Jesus Christ came into the world to save sinners. I'm proof—Public Sinner Number One—of someone who could never have made it apart from sheer mercy. And now he shows me off—evidence of his endless patience—to those who are right on the edge of trusting him forever.

1 TIMOTHY 1:15–16 THE MESSAGE

How can I
overcome temptation?

I have set before you life and death, blessing and cursing; therefore choose life, that both you and your descendants may live; that you may love the Lord your God, that you may obey His voice, and that you may cling to Him, for He is your life.

DEUTERONOMY 30:19–20 NKJV

Remember this—the wrong desires that come into your life aren't anything new and different. Many others have faced exactly the same problems before you. And no temptation is irresistible. You can trust God to keep the temptation from becoming so strong that you can't stand up against it, for he has promised this and will do what he says. He will show you how to escape temptation's power so that you can bear up patiently against it.

1 CORINTHIANS 10:13 TLB

— INSTRUCTIONS —

Happy is the man who doesn't give in and do wrong when he is tempted, for afterwards he will get as his reward the crown

of life that God has promised those who love him. And remember, when someone wants to do wrong it is never God who is tempting him, for God never wants to do wrong and never tempts anyone else to do it. Temptation is the pull of man's own evil thoughts and wishes. These evil thoughts lead to evil actions.

JAMES 1:12–15 TLB

How blessed is the man who does not walk in the counsel of the wicked, nor stand in the path of sinners, nor sit in the seat of scoffers! But his delight is in the law of the Lord, and in His law he meditates day and night. He will be like a tree firmly planted by streams of water, which yields its fruit in its season and its leaf does not wither; and in whatever he does, he prospers.

PSALM 1:1–3 NASB

If you want to enjoy life and see many happy days, keep your tongue from speaking evil and keep your lips from telling lies. Turn away from evil and do good. Search for peace, and work to maintain it. The eyes of the Lord watch over those who do right, and his ears are open to their prayers. But the Lord turns his face against those who do evil.

1 PETER 3:10–12 NLT

The good man does not escape all troubles— he has them too. But the Lord helps him in each and every one.

PSALM 34:19 TLB

The steps of good men are directed by the Lord. He delights in each step they take. If they fall it isn't fatal, for the Lord holds them with his hand.

PSALM 37:23–24 TLB

Be on your guard and stay awake. Your enemy, the devil, is like a roaring lion, sneaking around to find someone to attack. But you must resist the devil and stay strong in your faith.

1 PETER 5:8–9 CEV

Put on the full armor of God so that you can fight against the devil's evil tricks. Our fight is not against people on earth but against . . . the spiritual powers of evil in the heavenly world. That is why you need to put on God's full armor. Then on the day of evil you will be able to stand strong. And when you have finished the whole fight, you will still be standing.

EPHESIANS 6:11–13 NCV

You are strong, and the word of God lives in you, and you have overcome the evil one.

1 JOHN 2:14 NIV

Thank God! He gives us victory over sin and death through our Lord Jesus Christ.

1 CORINTHIANS 15:57 NLT

For every child of God can obey him, defeating sin and evil pleasure by trusting Christ to help him.

1 JOHN 5:4 TLB

Sin didn't, and doesn't, have a chance in competition with the aggressive forgiveness we call grace. When it's sin versus grace, grace wins hands down. All sin can do is threaten us with death, and that's the end of it. Grace, because God is putting everything together again through the Messiah, invites us into life—a life that goes on and on and on, world without end.

ROMANS 5:20–21 THE MESSAGE

— PROMISES —

The Lord knows how to deliver the godly out of temptations.

2 PETER 2:9 NKJV

The Lord is faithful, and He will strengthen and protect you from the evil one.

2 THESSALONIANS 3:3 NASB

You are from God, little children, and have overcome them; because greater is He who is in you than he who is in the world.

1 JOHN 4:4 NASB

I can do everything through Christ, who gives me strength.

PHILIPPIANS 4:13 NLT

God is the one who began this good work in you, and I am certain that he won't stop before it is complete on the day that Christ Jesus returns.

PHILIPPIANS 1:6 CEV

These trials are only to test your faith, to see whether or not it is strong and pure. It is being tested as fire tests gold and purifies it—and your faith is far more precious to God than mere gold; so if your faith remains strong after being tried in the test tube of fiery trials, it will bring you much praise and glory and honor on the day of his return.

1 PETER 1:7 TLB

All glory to God, who is able, through his mighty power at work within in us, to accomplish infinitely more than we might ask or think.

EPHESIANS 3:20 NLT

God can do anything, you know—far more than you could ever imagine or guess or request in your wildest dreams! He does it not by pushing us around but by working within us, his Spirit deeply and gently within us.

EPHESIANS 3:20 THE MESSAGE

[Not in your own strength] for it is God Who is all the while effectually at work in you [energizing and creating in you the power and desire] both to will and to work for His good pleasure and satisfaction and delight.

PHILIPPIANS 2:13 AMP

Anyone who meets a testing challenge head-on and manages to stick it out is mighty fortunate. For such persons loyally in love with God, the reward is life and more life.

JAMES 1:12 THE MESSAGE

I know how great this makes you feel, even though you have to put up with every kind of aggravation in the meantime. Pure gold put in the fire comes out of it proved pure; genuine faith put through this suffering comes out proved genuine. When Jesus wraps this all up, it's your faith, not your gold, that God will have on display as evidence of his victory.

1 PETER 1:6–7 THE MESSAGE

— PRAYERS —

Deliver us from the evil one.

MATTHEW 6:13 NKJV

The Lord will deliver me from every evil work and preserve me for His heavenly kingdom.

2 TIMOTHY 4:18 NKJV

Watch with me and pray lest the Tempter overpower you. For though the spirit is willing enough, the body is weak.

MARK 14:38 TLB

We always pray for you, asking our God to help you live the kind of life he called you to live. We pray that with his power God will help you do the good things you want and perform the works that come from your faith. We pray all this so that the name of our Lord Jesus Christ will have glory in you, and you will have glory in him.

2 THESSALONIANS 1:11–12 NCV

I lost my temper—again.
Help, Lord!

People with understanding control their anger; a hot temper shows great foolishness.

PROVERBS 14:29 NLT

Slowness to anger makes for deep understanding; a quick-tempered person stockpiles stupidity.

PROVERBS 14:29 THE MESSAGE

— INSTRUCTIONS —

Put these things out of your life: anger, bad temper, doing or saying things to hurt others, and using evil words when you talk.

COLOSSIANS 3:8 NCV

I promise you that on the day of judgment, everyone will have to account for every careless word they have spoken.

MATTHEW 12:36 CEV

You're familiar with the command to the ancients, "Do not murder." I'm telling you that anyone who is so much as angry with a brother or sister is guilty of murder. . . . The simple moral fact is that words kill.

MATTHEW 5:21–22 THE MESSAGE

Don't sin by letting anger control you. Don't let the sun go down while you are still angry, for anger gives a foothold to the devil.

EPHESIANS 4:26–27 NLT

When you talk, do not say harmful things, but say what people need—words that will help others become stronger. Then what you say will do good to those who listen to you.

EPHESIANS 4:29 NCV

Let every man be quick to hear [a ready listener], slow to speak, slow to take offense and to get angry. For man's anger does not promote the righteousness God [wishes and requires].

JAMES 1:19–20 AMP

God's righteousness doesn't grow from human anger.

JAMES 1:20 THE MESSAGE

Do not be overcome by evil, but overcome evil with good.

ROMANS 12:21 NASB

Since God chose you to be the holy people he loves, you must clothe yourselves with tenderhearted mercy, kindness, humility, gentleness, and patience. Make allowance for each other's faults, and forgive anyone who offends you. Remember, the Lord forgave you, so you must forgive others.

COLOSSIANS 3:12–13 NLT

— PROMISES —

We have everything we need to live a life that pleases
God. It was all given to us by God's own power, when
we learned that he had invited us to share in his wonderful goodness. God made great and marvelous promises,
so that his nature would become part of us. . . . Do your
best to improve your faith. You can do this by adding
goodness, understanding, self-control, patience, devotion to God.

2 Peter 1:3–6 cev

So make every effort to apply the benefits of these
promises to your life. . . . Knowing God leads to self-
control. Self-control leads to patient endurance, and
patient endurance leads to godliness.

2 Peter 1:5–6 nlt

Blessed are the merciful, for they shall receive
mercy. . . . Blessed are the peacemakers, for they
shall be called sons of God.

Matthew 5:7, 9 nasb

Delight yourself also in the Lord, and He will give you
the desires and secret petitions of your heart. Commit
your way to the Lord [roll and repose each care of your
load on Him]; trust (lean on, rely on, and be confident)
also in Him, and He will bring it to pass. . . .
Be still and rest in the Lord; wait for Him
and patiently lean yourself upon Him. . . .
Cease from anger and forsake wrath;

fret not yourself—it tends only to evil-doing. . . . But the meek [in the end] shall inherit the earth, and shall delight themselves in the abundance of peace.

PSALM 37:4–5, 7–8, 11 AMP

— PRAYER —

Who can understand his errors? Cleanse me from secret faults. Keep back Your servant also from presumptuous sins; let them not have dominion over me. Then I shall be blameless, and I shall be innocent of great transgression. Let the words of my mouth and the meditation of my heart be acceptable in Your sight, O Lord, my strength and my Redeemer.

PSALM 19:12–14 NKJV

We always pray that God will show you everything he wants you to do and that you may have all the wisdom and understanding that his Spirit gives. Then you will live a life that honors the Lord.

COLOSSIANS 1:9–10 CEV

— EXAMPLE —

Our Heavenly Father sees our failures and weakness yet responds with mercy and not anger:

The Lord is merciful and gracious, slow to anger, and plenteous in mercy and loving-kindness. He will not always chide or be contending, neither will He keep His anger for ever or hold a grudge. He has not dealt with us after our sins, nor rewarded us according to our iniquities. . . . As a father loves and pities his children, so the Lord loves and pities those who fear Him [with reverence, worship and awe]. For He knows our frame; He [earnestly] remembers and imprints [on His heart] that we are dust.

PSALM 103:8–10, 13–14 AMP

It's been a tough day, Lord. Do you have any words of encouragement?

Do not fear, for I am with you; do not anxiously look about you, for I am your God. I will strengthen you, surely I will help you, surely I will uphold you with My righteous right hand.

ISAIAH 41:10 NASB

Whatever I have, wherever I am, I can make it through anything in the One who makes me who I am.

PHILIPPIANS 4:13 THE MESSAGE

— INSTRUCTIONS —

Cast your burden upon the Lord and He will sustain you; He will never allow the righteous to be shaken.

PSALM 55:22 NASB

Fix your thoughts on what is true and good and right. Think about things that are pure and lovely, and dwell on the fine, good things in others. Think about all you can praise God for and be glad about. Keep putting into practice all you learned from me . . . and the God of peace will be with you.

PHILIPPIANS 4:8–9 TLB

Let the peace of heart that comes from Christ be always present in your hearts and lives. . . . And always be thankful.

COLOSSIANS 3:15 TLB

Let us hold unswervingly to the hope we profess, for he who promised is faithful.

HEBREWS 10:23 NIV

We fix our eyes not on what is seen, but on what is unseen. For what is seen is temporary, but what is unseen is eternal.

2 CORINTHIANS 4:18 NIV

We live by faith, not by sight.

2 CORINTHIANS 5:7 NIV

Now faith is being sure of what we hope for and certain of what we do not see.

HEBREWS 11:1 NIV

Even though on the outside it often looks like things are falling apart on us, on the inside, where God is making new life, not a day goes by without his unfolding grace.

2 CORINTHIANS 4:16 THE MESSAGE

We are like clay jars in which this treasure is stored. The real power comes from God and not from us. Even when we don't know what to do, we never give up. In times of trouble, God is with us, and when we are knocked down, we get up again.

2 CORINTHIANS 4:7–9 CEV

We felt like we'd been sent to death row, that it was all over for us. As it turned out, it was the best thing that could have happened. Instead of trusting in our own strength or wits to get out of it, we were forced to trust God totally—not a bad idea since he's the God who raises the dead!

2 CORINTHIANS 1:9 THE MESSAGE

— PROMISES —

He gives power to the faint and weary, and to him who has no might He increases strength [causing it to multiply and making it abound].

ISAIAH 40:29 AMP

Nothing you do for him is a waste of time or effort.

1 CORINTHIANS 15:58 THE MESSAGE

And I am sure that God, who began the good work within you, will continue his work until it is finally finished on that day when Christ Jesus comes back again.

PHILIPPIANS 1:6 NLT

Be energetic in your life of salvation, reverent and sensitive before God. That energy is God's energy, an energy deep within you, God himself willing and working at what will give him the most pleasure.

PHILIPPIANS 2:12–13 THE MESSAGE

— PRAYERS —

We pray that you'll have the strength to stick it out over the long haul . . . strength that endures the unendurable and spills over into joy.

COLOSSIANS 1:11–12 THE MESSAGE

We wait in hope for the Lord; he is our help and our shield. In him our hearts rejoice, for we trust in his holy name. May your unfailing love rest upon us, O Lord, even as we put our hope in you.

PSALM 33:20–22 NIV

I wait for the Lord, my soul does wait, and in His word do I hope. My soul waits for the Lord more than the watchmen for the morning. . . . Hope in the Lord; for with the Lord there is lovingkindness, and with Him is abundant redemption.

PSALM 130:5–7 NASB

When You said, "Seek My face," my heart said to You, "Your face, O Lord, I shall seek." I would have despaired unless I had believed that I would see the goodness of the Lord in the land of the living.

PSALM 27:8, 13 NASB

Now to Him who is able to keep you from stumbling, and to make you stand in the presence of His glory blameless with great joy, to the only God our Savior, through Jesus Christ our Lord, be glory, majesty, dominion and authority.

JUDE 24–25 NASB

— EXAMPLE —

God gave each of us certain "gifts" to keep us aware of our constant need to rely on His strength rather than our own:

Satan's angel did his best to get me down; what he in fact did was push me to my knees. No danger then of walking around high and mighty! At first I didn't think of it as a gift, and begged God to remove it. Three times I did that, and then he told me, "My grace is enough; it's all you need. My strength comes into its own in your weakness." . . . It was a case of Christ's strength moving in on my weakness. Now I take limitations in stride, and with good cheer. . . . I just let Christ take over! And so the weaker I get, the stronger I become.

2 CORINTHIANS 12:7–10 THE MESSAGE

Lord, I know you can heal me. Will you? What is my part in the process?

The Lord says, "I will rescue those who love me. I will protect those who trust in my name. When they call on me, I will answer; I will be with them in trouble. I will rescue and honor them. I will satisfy them with a long life and give them my salvation."

PSALM 91:14–16 NLT

I am the Lord that healeth thee.

EXODUS 15:26 KJV

— INSTRUCTIONS —

Trust in the Lord with all your heart and do not lean on your own understanding. In all your ways acknowledge Him, and He will make your paths straight. Do not be wise in your own eyes; fear the Lord and turn away from evil. It will be healing to your body and refreshment to your bones.

PROVERBS 3:5–8 NASB

My child, pay attention to what I say. Listen carefully to my words. Don't lose sight of them. Let them penetrate deep into your heart, for they bring life to those who find them, and healing to their whole body.

PROVERBS 4:20–22 NLT

Is any one of you sick? He should call the elders of the church to pray over him and anoint him with oil in the name of the Lord. And the prayer offered in faith will make the sick person well; the Lord will raise him up. If he has sinned, he will be forgiven. Therefore confess your sins to each other and pray for each other so that you may be healed. The prayer of a righteous man is powerful and effective.

JAMES 5:14–16 NIV

These signs will follow those who believe: In My name they will cast out demons . . . they will lay hands on the sick, and they will recover.

MARK 16:17–18 NKJV

I tell you the truth, anyone who believes in me will do the same works I have done, and even greater works, because I am going to be with the Father. You can ask for anything in my name, and I will do it, so that the Son can bring glory to the Father.

JOHN 14:12–13 NLT

God's love, though, is ever and always,
eternally present to all who fear him,
making every thing right for them

and their children as they follow his Covenant ways and remember to do whatever he said.

PSALM 103:17–18 THE MESSAGE

Oh, give thanks to the Lord! Call upon His name; make known His deeds among the peoples! Sing to Him, sing psalms to Him; talk of all His wondrous works! Glory in His holy name; let the hearts of those rejoice who who seek the Lord! Seek the Lord and His strength; seek His face evermore! Remember His marvelous works which He has done, His wonders, and the judgments of His mouth. . . . He remembers His covenant forever, the word which He commanded, for a thousand generations.

PSALM 105:1–8 NKJV

Never give up praying. And when you pray, keep alert and be thankful.

COLOSSIANS 4:2 CEV

— PROMISES —

Jesus Christ never changes! He is the same yesterday, today, and forever.

HEBREWS 13:8 CEV

Of all the people on earth, the Lord your God has chosen you to be his own special treasure. . . . He is the faithful God who keeps his covenant for a thousand generations and lavishes his unfailing love on those who love him and obey his commands. . . . He will love you and bless you. . . . And the Lord will protect you from all sickness.

DEUTERONOMY 7:6, 9, 13, 15 NLT

"I will restore you to health and heal your wounds," declares the Lord.

JEREMIAH 30:17 NIV

He suffered and endured great pain for us, but we thought his suffering was punishment from God. But he was wounded and crushed because of our sins; by taking our punishment, he made us completely well.

ISAIAH 53:4–5 CEV

Christ carried the burden of our sins. He was nailed to the cross, so that we would stop sinning and start living right. By his cuts and bruises you are healed.

1 PETER 2:24 CEV

Worship only me, the Lord your God! I will bless you with plenty of food and water and keep you strong.

EXODUS 23:25 CEV

Jesus said to him, "I will go and heal him."

MATTHEW 8:7 NIV

He sent forth his word and healed them; he rescued them from the grave.

PSALM 107:20 NIV

Be strong and of good courage, do not fear nor be afraid of them; for the Lord your God, He is the One who goes with you. He will not leave you nor forsake you.

DEUTERONOMY 31:6 NKJV

— PRAYERS —

What shall I render to the Lord for all His benefits toward me? I will take up the cup of salvation, and call upon the name of the Lord. . . . I will offer to You the sacrifice of thanksgiving, and will call upon the name of the Lord.

PSALM 116:12–13, 17 NKJV

Oh my soul, bless God, don't forget a single blessing! He forgives your sins—every one. He heals your diseases—every one.

PSALM 103:2–3 THE MESSAGE

Heal me, O Lord, and I will be healed; save me and I will be saved, for you are the one I praise.

JEREMIAH 17:14 NIV

Lord, how you have helped me before! You took me safely from my mother's womb and brought me through the years of infancy. I have depended upon you since birth; you have always been my God. Don't leave me now, for trouble is near and no one else can possibly help.

PSALM 22:9–11 TLB

I pray that God, who gives peace, will make you completely holy. And may your spirit, soul, and body be kept healthy and faultless until our Lord Jesus returns. The one who chose you can be trusted, and he will do this.

1 THESSALONIANS 5:23–24 CEV

He is my God, and I am trusting him. For he rescues you from every trap, and protects you from the fatal plague. He will shield you with his wings! They will shelter you. His faithful promises are your armor.

PSALM 91:2–4 TLB

In your day of trouble, may the Lord be with you! May the God of Jacob keep you from all harm. . . . May there be shouts of joy when we hear the news of your victory, flags flying with praise to God for all that he has done for you.

PSALM 20:1, 5 TLB

Whatever you ask for in prayer, believe that you have received it, and it will be yours.

MARK 11:24 NIV

— EXAMPLES —

There are many examples in the Bible of people asking for—and receiving—healing. Here are three:

As Jesus went on from there, two blind men followed him, calling out, "Have mercy on us, Son of David!" When he had gone indoors, the blind men came to him, and he asked them, "Do you believe that I am able to do this?" "Yes, Lord," they replied. Then he touched their eyes and said, "According to your faith will it be done to you."

MATTHEW 9:27–29 NIV

A man with leprosy came and knelt before him and said, "Lord, if you are willing, you can make me clean." Jesus reached out his hand and touched the man. "I am willing," he said. "Be clean!" Immediately he was cured of his leprosy.

MATTHEW 8:2–3 NIV

One of them, when he saw he was healed, came back, praising God in a loud voice. He threw himself at Jesus' feet and thanked him—and he was a Samaritan. Jesus asked, "Were not all ten cleansed? Where are the other nine? Was no one found to return and give praise to God except this foreigner?" Then he said to him, "Rise and go; your faith has made you well."

LUKE 17:15–19 NIV

Lord, I've prayed, but I don't see any changes. What more can I do?

Trust in the Lord, and do good; dwell in the land, and feed on His faithfulness. Delight yourself also in the Lord, and He shall give you the desires of your heart. Commit your way to the Lord, trust also in Him, and He shall bring it to pass. . . . Rest in the Lord, and wait patiently for Him.

PSALM 37:3–5, 7 NKJV

— INSTRUCTIONS —

You need to persevere so that when you have done the will of God, you will receive what he has promised.

HEBREWS 10:36 NIV

Therefore, take up the full armor of God, so that you may be able to resist in the evil day, and having done everything, to stand firm.

EPHESIANS 6:13 NASB

Stand firm. Let nothing move you. Always give yourselves fully to the work of the Lord, because you know that your labor in the Lord is not in vain.

1 CORINTHIANS 15:58 NIV

Wait . . . for God. Wait with hope. Hope now; hope always!

PSALM 131:3 THE MESSAGE

"Have faith in God," Jesus answered. "I tell you the truth, if anyone says to this mountain, 'Go, throw yourself into the sea,' and does not doubt in his heart but believes that what he says will happen, it will be done for him. Therefore I tell you, whatever you ask for in prayer, believe that you have received it, and it will be yours."

MARK 11:22–24 NIV

We're not giving up. How could we! Even though on the outside it often looks like things are falling apart on us, on the inside, where God is making new life, not a day goes by without his unfolding grace. . . . There's far more here than meets the eye. The things we see now are here today, gone tomorrow. But the things we can't see now will last forever.

2 CORINTHIANS 4:16, 18 THE MESSAGE

Be like those who through faith and patience will receive what God has promised.

HEBREWS 6:12 NCV

Stay with God! Take heart. Don't quit.
I'll say it again: Stay with God.

PSALM 27:14 THE MESSAGE

— PRAYERS —

May the God of hope fill you with all joy and peace as you trust in him, so that you may overflow with hope by the power of the Holy Spirit.

ROMANS 15:13 NIV

We pray that you'll have the strength to stick it out over the long haul—not the grim strength of gritting your teeth but the glory-strength God gives. It is strength that endures the unendurable and spills over into joy.

COLOSSIANS 1:11 THE MESSAGE

— PROMISES —

Everything that was written in the past was written to teach us. The Scriptures give us patience and encouragement so that we can have hope. Patience and encouragement come from God.

ROMANS 15:4–5 NCV

He gives power to the faint and weary, and to him who has no might He increases strength [causing it to multiply and making it to abound]. . . . Those who wait for the Lord [who expect, look for, and hope in Him] shall change and renew their strength and power; they shall lift their wings and mount up [close to God] as eagles [mount up to the sun]; they shall run and not be weary, they shall walk and not faint or become tired.

ISAIAH 40:29, 31 AMP

Don't worry about anything; instead, pray about everything. Tell God what you need, and thank him for all he has done. Then you will experience God's peace, which exceeds anything we can understand. His peace will guard your hearts and minds as you live in Christ Jesus.

PHILIPPIANS 4:6–7 NLT

The earnest (heartfelt, continued) prayer of a righteous man makes tremendous power available [dynamic in its working].

JAMES 5:16 AMP

When God made his promise to Abraham, he backed it to the hilt, putting his own reputation on the line. He said, "I promise that I'll bless you with everything I have. . . ." Abraham stuck it out and got everything that had been promised to him. When God wanted to guarantee his promises, he gave his word, a rock-solid guarantee— God can't break his word. And because his word cannot change, the promise is likewise unchangeable. We who have run for our very lives to God have every reason to grab the promised hope with both hands and never let go. It's an unbreakable spiritual lifeline, reaching past all appearances right to the very presence of God.

HEBREWS 6:13-14, 17–19 THE MESSAGE

We continue to shout our praise even when we're hemmed in with troubles, because we know how troubles can develop passionate patience in us, and how that patience in turn forges the tempered steel of virtue, keeping us alert for whatever God will do next.

ROMANS 5:3–4 THE MESSAGE

— EXAMPLE —

Abraham kept believing God's promise to him, no matter what he saw or felt:

There was no hope that Abraham would have children. But Abraham believed God and continued hoping, and so he became the father of many nations. As God told him, "Your descendants also will be too many to count." Abraham was almost a hundred years old, much past the age for having children, and Sarah could not have children. Abraham thought about all this, but his faith in God did not become weak. He never doubted that God would keep his promise, and he never stopped believing. He grew stronger in his faith and gave praise to God. Abraham felt sure that God was able to do what he had promised.

ROMANS 4:18–21 NCV

And so after waiting patiently, Abraham received what was promised.

HEBREWS 6:15 NIV

Lord, I'm having trouble paying my bills. Do you have any advice for me?

I will instruct you and teach you in the way which you should go; I will counsel you with My eye upon you.

PSALM 32:8 NASB

I am the Lord your God, who teaches you to profit, who leads you in the way you should go.

ISAIAH 48:17 NASB

The reward of humility and the fear of the Lord are riches, honor and life.

PROVERBS 22:4 NASB

— INSTRUCTIONS —

How blessed is the man who fears the Lord, who greatly delights in His commandments. . . . Wealth and riches are in his house, and his righteousness endures forever.

PSALM 112:1, 3 NASB

In everything you do, put God first, and he will direct you and crown your efforts with success.

PROVERBS 3:6 TLB

So don't worry about these things, saying, "What will we eat? What will we drink? What will we wear?" These things dominate the thoughts of unbelievers, but your heavenly Father already knows all your needs. Seek the Kingdom of God above all else, and live righteously, and he will give you everything you need. So don't worry about tomorrow, for tomorrow will bring its own worries. Today's trouble is enough for today.

MATTHEW 6:31–34 NLT

This Book of the Law shall not depart from your mouth, but you shall meditate in it day and night, that you may observe to do according to all that is written in it. For then you will make your way prosperous, and then you will have good success. . . . Be strong and of good courage; do not be afraid, nor be dismayed, for the Lord your God is with you wherever you go.

JOSHUA 1:8–9 NKJV

Lazy hands make a man poor, but diligent hands bring wealth.

PROVERBS 10:4 NIV

The sluggard craves and gets nothing, but the desires of the diligent are fully satisfied.

PROVERBS 13:4 NIV

He who tills his land will have plenty of food, but he who follows empty pursuist will have poverty in plenty.

PROVERBS 28:19 NASB

Lust for money brings trouble and nothing but trouble. Going down that path, some lose their footing in the faith completely and live to regret it bitterly ever after.

1 TIMOTHY 6:10 THE MESSAGE

Don't be obsessed with getting more material things.

HEBREWS 13:5 THE MESSAGE

You can't worship two gods at once. Loving one god, you'll end up hating the other. Adoration of one feeds contempt for the other. You can't worship God and Money both.

MATTHEW 6:24 THE MESSAGE

But you shall remember the Lord your God, for it is He who is giving you power to make wealth, that He may confirm His covenant which He swore to your fathers, as it is this day.

DEUTERONOMY 8:18 NASB

Honor the Lord by giving him the first part of all your income, and he will fill your barns with wheat and barley and overflow your wine vats with the finest wines.

PROVERBS 3:9–10 TLB

"Bring all the tithes into the storehouse so there will be enough food in my Temple. If you do," says the Lord of Heaven's Armies, "I will open the windows of heaven for you. I will pour out a blessing so great you won't have enough room to take it in! Try it! Put me to the test!"

MALACHI 3:10 NLT

— PROMISES —

For the Lord gives wisdom; from His mouth come knowledge and understanding; He stores up sound wisdom for the upright; He is a shield to those who walk uprightly; He guards the paths of justice, and preserves the way of His saints.

PROVERBS 2:6–8 NKJV

The Lord will guide you continually, and satisfy your soul in drought, and strengthen your bones; you shall be like a watered garden, and like a spring of water, whose waters do not fail.

ISAIAH 58:11 NKJV

I have been young and now I am old. And in all my years I have never seen the Lord forsake a man who loves him; nor have I seen the children of the godly go hungry.

PSALM 37:25–26 TLB

For if you give, you will get! Your gift will return to you in full and overflowing measure, pressed down, shaken together to make room for more, and running over. Whatever measure you use to give—large or small— will be used to measure what is given back to you.

LUKE 6:38 TLB

Mercy to the needy is a loan to God, and God pays back those loans in full.

PROVERBS 19:17 THE MESSAGE

Good will come to him who is generous and lends freely, who conducts his affairs with justice. Surely he will never be shaken; a righteous man will be remembered forever. He will have no fear of bad news; his heart is steadfast, trusting in the Lord. . . . In the end he will look in triumph on his foes.

PSALM 112:5–9 NIV

Those who seek the Lord shall not lack any good thing.

PSALM 34:10 NKJV

The blessing of the Lord makes one rich, and He adds no sorrow with it.

PROVERBS 10:22 NKJV

This same God who takes care of me will supply all your needs from his glorious riches, which have been given to us in Christ Jesus.

PHILIPPIANS 4:19 NLT

— PRAYERS —

The Lord be magnified, who delights in the prosperity of His servant.

PSALM 35:27 NASB

Both riches and honor come from You, and You rule over all, and in Your hand is power and might; and it lies in Your hand to make great and to strengthen everyone.

1 CHRONICLES 29:12 NASB

In you, O Lord, I have taken refuge; let me never be put to shame; deliver me in your righteousness. Turn your ear to me, come quickly to my rescue; be my rock of refuge, a strong fortress to save me. Since you are my rock and my fortress, for the sake of your name lead and guide me. Free me from the trap that is set for me, for you are my refuge.

PSALM 31:1–4 NIV

Though I walk in the midst of trouble, you preserve my life; you stretch out your hand against the anger of my foes, with your right hand you save me. The Lord will fulfill his purpose for me.

PSALM 138:7–8 NIV

My lies are catching up with me. How can I quit? It's hard to always tell the truth.

Lovingly follow the truth at all times—speaking truly, dealing truly, living truly—and so become more and more in every way like Christ.

EPHESIANS 4:15 TLB

— INSTRUCTIONS —

Be an example . . . with your words, your actions, your love, your faith, and your pure life.

1 TIMOTHY 4:12 NCV

Tell your neighbor the truth. . . . When you lie to others, you end up lying to yourself.

EPHESIANS 4:25 THE MESSAGE

An honest life shows respect for God; a degenerate life is a slap in his face.

PROVERBS 14:2 THE MESSAGE

Stop lying to each other. You have given up your old way of life with its habits. Each of you is now a new person. You are becoming more and more like your Creator.

COLOSSIANS 3:9–10 CEV

Truth will last forever; lies are soon found out.

PROVERBS 12:19 CEV

The person who tells lies gets caught; the person who spreads rumors is ruined.

PROVERBS 19:9 THE MESSAGE

If you do the right thing, honesty will be your guide. But if you are crooked, you will be trapped by your own dishonesty.

PROVERBS 11:3 CEV

These liars have lied so well and for so long that they've lost their capacity for truth.

1 TIMOTHY 4:2 THE MESSAGE

— PROMISES —

Do you want to live and enjoy a long life? Then don't say cruel things and don't tell lies. Do good instead of evil and try to live at peace. If you obey the Lord, he will watch over you and answer your prayers. But God despises evil people, and he will wipe them all from the earth, till they are forgotten. When his people pray for help, he listens and rescues them from their troubles.

PSALM 34:12–17 CEV

If anyone is in Christ, he is a new creation; old things have passed away; behold, all things have become new.

2 CORINTHIANS 5:17 NKJV

God is working in you to make you willing and able to obey him.

PHILIPPIANS 2:13 CEV

— PRAYERS —

You deserve honesty from the heart; yes, utter sincerity and truthfulness. . . . Create in me a new, clean heart, O God, filled with clean thoughts and right desires.

PSALM 51:6, 10 TLB

We have continued praying for you, asking God that you will know fully what he wants. We pray that you will also have great wisdom and understanding in spiritual things so that you will live the kind of life that honors and pleases the Lord in every way. . . . God has freed us from the power of darkness, and he brought us into the kingdom of his dear Son.

COLOSSIANS 1:9–10, 13 NCV

— EXAMPLES —

There are many accounts in the Bible of people lying. Notice how each of these lies brought consequences:

Peter began to curse and swear, "I don't know that man!" Right then a rooster crowed, and Peter remembered that Jesus had said, "Before a rooster crows, you will

say three times that you don't know me." Then Peter
went out and cried hard.

MATTHEW 26:74–75 CEV

Elisha said to him, "Where did you go, Gehazi?" And
he said, "Your servant did not go anywhere." Then
he said to him . . . "Is it time to receive money and to
receive clothing, olive groves and vineyards, sheep and
oxen, male and female servants? Therefore the leprosy
of Naaman shall cling to you and your descendants
forever." And he went out from his presence leprous, as
white as snow.

2 KINGS 5:25–27 NKJV

Now it was about three hours later when his wife came
in, not knowing what had happened. And Peter answered
her, "Tell me whether you sold the land for so much?"
She said, "Yes, for so much." Then Peter said to her,
"How is it that you have agreed together to test the Spirit
of the Lord? Look, the feet of those who have buried
your husband are at the door, and they will carry you
out." Then immediately she fell down at his feet and
breathed her last.

ACTS 5:7–10 NKJV

I know I need to take a stand for what is right. But how will I handle the persecution?

Fear not, for I am with you; be not dismayed, for I am your God. I will strengthen you, yes, I will help you, I will uphold you with My righteous right hand. Behold, all those who were incensed against you shall be ashamed and disgraced.

ISAIAH 41:10–11 NKJV

For the Lord God helps Me; therefore have I not been ashamed or confounded; therefore have I set My face like a flint, and I know that I shall not be put to shame.

ISAIAH 50:7 AMP

— INSTRUCTIONS —

Be an example to the believers with your words, your actions, your love, your faith, and your pure life.

1 TIMOTHY 4:12 NCV

You're blessed when your commitment to God provokes persecution. The persecution drives you even deeper into God's kingdom. Not only that—count yourselves blessed every time people put you down or throw you out or speak lies about you to discredit me. What it means is that the truth is too close for comfort and they are uncomfortable. You can be glad when that happens—give a cheer, even!—for though they don't like it, I do! And all heaven applauds. And know that you are in good company. My prophets and witnesses have always gotten into this kind of trouble.

MATTHEW 5:10–12 THE MESSAGE

There's trouble ahead when you live only for the approval of others, saying what flatters them, doing what indulges them. Popularity contests are not truth contests. . . . Your task is to be true, not popular.

LUKE 6:26 THE MESSAGE

For I am not ashamed of the gospel of Christ, for it is the power of God to salvation for everyone who believes.

ROMANS 1:16 NKJV

This is why we work hard and continue to struggle, for our hope is in the living God, who is the Savior of all people and particularly of those who believe.

1 TIMOTHY 4:10 NLT

Stay away from foolish and stupid arguments, because you know they grow into quarrels. And a servant of the Lord must not quarrel but must be kind to everyone, a good teacher, and patient. The Lord's servant must gently teach those who disagree.

2 TIMOTHY 2:23–25 NCV

Take into your heart all My words which I will speak to you and listen closely. Go to . . . the sons of your people, and speak to them and tell them, whether they listen or not.

EZEKIEL 3:10–11 NASB

Bless those who persecute you. Don't curse them; pray that God will bless them.

ROMANS 12:14 NLT

Speak up for the right living that goes along with true Christianity. . . . And here you yourself must be an example to them of good deeds of every kind. Let everything you do reflect your love of the truth and the fact that you are in dead earnest about it.

TITUS 2:1, 7 TLB

Put on the full armor of God, so that when the day of evil comes, you may be able to stand your ground.

EPHESIANS 6:13 NIV

— PROMISES —

You are of God, little children, and have overcome them, because He who is in you is greater than he who is in the world.

1 JOHN 4:4 NKJV

Fear of man will prove to be a snare, but whoever trusts in the Lord is kept safe.

PROVERBS 29:25 NIV

He Himself has said, "I will never leave you nor forsake you." So we may boldly say: "The Lord is my helper; I will not fear. What can man do to me?"

HEBREWS 13:5–6 NKJV

I give you peace, the kind of peace that only I can give. It isn't like the peace that this world can give. So don't be worried or afraid.

JOHN 14:27 CEV

— PRAYERS —

Show that I am right, Lord! I stay true to myself, and I have trusted you without doubting. Test my thoughts and find out what I am like. I never forget your kindness, and I am always faithful to you. I don't spend time with worthless liars or go with evil crowds.

PSALM 26:1–5 CEV

The Lord is my light and my salvation; whom shall I fear? The Lord is the strength of my life; of whom shall I be afraid?

PSALM 27:1 NKJV

If God is for us, who can be against us?

ROMANS 8:31 NKJV

May the God of peace himself make you entirely pure and devoted to God; and may your spirit and soul and body be

kept strong and blameless until that day when our Lord
Jesus Christ comes back again.

1 THESSALONIANS 5:23 TLB

— EXAMPLE —

*Shadrach, Meshach, and Abednego stood together
against tremendous pressure. Because they steadfastly
refused to bow down and worship the golden idol, God
protected and promoted them:*

The fire hadn't touched them—not a hair of their heads
was singed; their coats were un-scorched, and they
didn't even smell of smoke! Then Nebuchadnezzar
said, "Blessed be the God of Shadrach, Meshach, and
Abednego, for he sent his angel to deliver his trusting
servants when they defied the king's commandment and
were willing to die rather than serve or worship any god
except their own." . . . Then the king gave promotions
to Shadrach, Meshach, and Abednego, so that they prospered greatly there in the province of Babylon.

DANIEL 3:27–28, 30 TLB

I am overwhelmed by my responsibilities. How can I cope with stress?

Do not let your hearts be troubled. Trust in God; trust also in me. . . . Peace I leave with you; my peace I give you. I do not give to you as the world gives. Do not let your hearts be troubled and do not be afraid.

JOHN 14:1, 27 NIV

Don't fret or worry. Instead of worrying, pray. Let petitions and praises shape your worries into prayers, letting God know your concerns. Before you know it, a sense of God's wholeness, everything coming together for good, will come and settle you down. It's wonderful what happens when Christ displaces worry at the center of your life.

PHILIPPIANS 4:6–8 THE MESSAGE

— INSTRUCTIONS —

Pile your troubles on God's shoulders—he'll carry your load, he'll help you out.

PSALM 55:22 THE MESSAGE

Come to me. Get away with me and you'll recover your life. I'll show you how to take a real rest. Walk with me and work with me—watch how I do it. Learn the unforced rhythms of grace. I won't lay anything heavy or ill-fitting on you. Keep company with me and you'll learn to live freely and lightly.

MATTHEW 11:28–30 THE MESSAGE

What I'm trying to do here is to get you to relax, to not be so preoccupied with getting, so you can respond to God's giving. People who don't know God and the way he works fuss over these things, but you know both God and how he works. Steep your life in God-reality, God-initiative, God-provisions. Don't worry about missing out. You'll find all your everyday human concerns will be met. Give your entire attention to what God is doing right now, and don't get worked up about what may or may not happen tomorrow. God will help you deal with whatever hard things come up when the time comes.

MATTHEW 6:31–34 THE MESSAGE

Here's what I want you to do: Find a quiet, secluded place so you won't be tempted to role-play before God. Just be there as simply and honestly as you can manage. The focus will shift from you to God, and you will begin to sense his grace.

MATTHEW 6:6 THE MESSAGE

This is the resting place, let the weary rest . . . This is the place of repose.

ISAIAH 28:12 NIV

— PRAYERS —

The minute I said, "I'm slipping, I'm falling," your love, God, took hold and held me fast. When I was upset and beside myself, you calmed me down and cheered me up.

PSALM 94:18–19 THE MESSAGE

You are my hiding place! You protect me from trouble, and you put songs in my heart because you have saved me.

PSALM 32:7 CEV

Teach me true wisdom.

PSALM 51:6 CEV

We also pray that you will be strengthened with his glorious power so that you will have all the endurance and patience you need. May you be filled with joy, always thanking the Father.

COLOSSIANS 1:11–12 NLT

— PROMISES —

I have told you these things, so that in me you may have peace. In this world you will have trouble. But take heart! I have overcome the world.

JOHN 16:33 NIV

I love you, O Lord, my strength. The Lord is my rock, my fortress and my deliverer; my God is my rock, in whom I take refuge. He is my shield and the horn of my salvation, my stronghold.

PSALM 18:1–2 NIV

A thousand may fall at your side, ten thousand at your right hand, but it will not come near you. . . . If you make the Most High your dwelling—even the Lord, who is my refuge—then no harm will befall you, no disaster will come near your tent.

PSALM 91:7, 9–10 NIV

No temptation has seized you except what is common to man. And God is faithful; he will not let you be tempted beyond what you can bear. But when you are tempted, he will also provide a way out so that you can stand up under it.

1 CORINTHIANS 10:13 NIV

How blessed the man you train, God, the woman you instruct in your Word, providing a circle of quiet within the clamor of evil.

PSALM 94:12–13 THE MESSAGE

When anxiety was great within me, your consolation brought joy to my soul.

PSALM 94:19 NIV

But those who hope in the Lord will renew their strength. They will soar on wings like eagles; they will run and not grow weary, they will walk and not be faint.

ISAIAH 40:31 NIV

Because the Sovereign Lord helps me, I will not be disgraced.

ISAIAH 50:7 NIV

I can do all things through Christ who strengthens me.

PHILIPPIANS 4:13 NKJV

If you need wisdom, ask our generous God, and he will give it to you. He will not rebuke you for asking.

JAMES 1:5 NLT

Wisdom and truth will enter the very center of your being, filling your life with joy.

PROVERBS 2:10 TLB

EXAMPLE

When Moses was overwhelmed with the responsibility of caring for the nation of Israel, God provided wisdom and a plan that took the pressure off:

What you are doing is not good. You and these people who come to you will only wear yourselves out. The work is too heavy for you; you cannot handle it alone. But select capable men from all the people . . . and appoint them as officials over thousands, hundreds, fifties and tens. That will make your load lighter, because they will share it with you.

EXODUS 18:17-18, 21–22 NIV

WHAT IS
THE SECRET
TO GOOD
RELATIONSHIPS?

I'm lonely, Lord.
Can you help me build lasting friendships?

Love from the center of who you are; don't fake it. Run for dear life from evil; hold on for dear life to good. Be good friends who love deeply.

ROMANS 12:9–10 THE MESSAGE

This is my prayer: that your love will flourish and that you will not only love much but well. Learn to love appropriately. You need to use your head and test your feelings so that your love is sincere and intelligent, not sentimental gush. Live a lover's life, circumspect and exemplary, a life Jesus will be proud of.

PHILIPPIANS 1:9–10 THE MESSAGE

— INSTRUCTIONS —

Watch what God does, and then you do it, like children who learn proper behavior from their parents. Mostly what God does is love you. Keep company with him and learn a life of love. Observe how Christ loved us. His love was not cautious but extravagant. He didn't love in order to get something from us but to give everything of himself to us. Love like that.

EPHESIANS 5:1–2 THE MESSAGE

Above all, love each other deeply, because love covers over a multitude of sins.

1 PETER 4:8 NIV

Put on a heart of compassion, kindness, humility, gentleness and patience; bearing with one another, and forgiving each other, whoever has a complaint against anyone; just as the Lord forgave you, so also should you. Beyond all these things put on love, which is the perfect bond of unity.

COLOSSIANS 3:12–14 NASB

You must quit being angry, hateful, and evil. You must no longer say insulting or cruel things about others. And stop lying to each other. You have given up your old way of life with its habits. Each of you is now a new person. You are becoming more and more like your Creator. . . . So be gentle, kind, humble, meek, and patient. Put up with each other, and forgive anyone who does you wrong, just as Christ has forgiven you.

COLOSSIANS 3:8–10, 12–13 CEV

Give as freely as you have received!

MATTHEW 10:8 NLT

Love endures long and is patient and kind; love never is envious nor boils over with jealousy; is not boastful or vainglorious, does not display itself haughtily. It is not conceited (arrogant and inflated with pride); it is not rude (unmannerly), and does not act unbecomingly. Love (God's love in us) does not insist on its own rights or its own way, for it is not self-seeking; it is not touchy or fretful or resentful; it takes no account of the evil done to it [pays no attention to a suffered wrong]. It does not rejoice at injustice and unrighteousness, but rejoices when right and truth prevail. Love bears up under anything and everything that comes, is ever ready to believe the best of every person, its hopes are fadeless under all circumstances and it endures everything [without weakening]. Love never fails [never fades out or becomes obsolete or comes to an end].

1 CORINTHIANS 13:4–8 AMP

Gently encourage the stragglers, and reach out for the exhausted, pulling them to their feet. Be patient with each person, attentive to individual needs. . . . Look for the best in each other, and always do your best to bring it out.

1 THESSALONIANS 5:14–15 THE MESSAGE

— PROMISES —

But the Holy Spirit produces this kind of fruit in our lives: love, joy, peace, patience, kindness, goodness, faithfulness, gentleness, and self-control.

GALATIANS 5:22–23 NLT

God has poured out his love into our hearts by the Holy Spirit, whom he has given us.

ROMANS 5:5 NIV

All who confess that Jesus is the Son of God have God living in them, and they live in God. . . . As we live in God, our love grows more perfect. . . . We love each other because he loved us first.

1 JOHN 4:15, 17, 19 NLT

— PRAYERS —

May the Lord make your love increase and overflow for each other and for everyone else, just as ours does for you.

1 THESSALONIANS 3:12 NIV

I pray that the Lord will guide you to be as loving as God and as patient as Christ.

2 THESSALONIANS 3:5 CEV

We pray that our Lord Jesus Christ and God our Father will encourage you and help you always to do and say the right thing.

2 THESSALONIANS 2:16–17 CEV

I pray that your love will overflow more and more, and that you will keep on growing in knowledge and understanding. For I want you to understand what really matters, so that you may live pure and blameless lives until the day of Christ's return. May you always be filled with the fruit of your salvation—the righteous character produced in your life by Jesus Christ.

PHILIPPIANS 1:9–11 NLT

— EXAMPLE —

God gave us the ultimate example of love:

This is how God showed his love for us: God sent his only Son into the world so we might live through him. . . . If God loved us like this, we certainly ought to love each other.

1 JOHN 4:9, 11 THE MESSAGE

If we love each other, God lives in us, and his love has been brought to full expression in us.

1 JOHN 4:12 NLT

What should I look for in a friend?

Pursue righteous living, faithfulness, love, and peace. Enjoy the companionship of those who call on the Lord with pure hearts.

2 TIMOTHY 2:22 NLT

I choose as my friends everyone who worships you and follows your teachings.

PSALM 119:63 CEV

— INSTRUCTIONS —

Wise friends make you wise, but you hurt yourself by going around with fools.

PROVERBS 13:20 CEV

Stay away from fools, for you won't find knowledge on their lips. The prudent understand where they are going, but fools deceive themselves. Fools make fun of guilt, but the godly acknowledge it and seek reconciliation.

PROVERBS 14:7–9 NLT

Friends come and friends go, but a true friend sticks by you like family.

PROVERBS 18:24 THE MESSAGE

The person who shuns the bitter moments of friends will be an outsider at their celebrations.

PROVERBS 14:10 THE MESSAGE

Don't make friends with anyone who has a bad temper. You might turn out like them and get caught in a trap.

PROVERBS 22:24–25 CEV

I am writing to tell you that you must not associate with those who call themselves believers in Christ but who sin sexually, or are greedy, or worship idols, or abuse others with words, or get drunk, or cheat people. Do not even eat with people like that.

1 CORINTHIANS 5:11 NCV

Don't team up with those who are unbelievers. How can righteousness be a partner with wickedness? How can light live with darkness? What harmony can there be between Christ and the devil? How can a believer be a partner with an unbeliever? And what union can there be between God's temple and idols? For we are the temple of the living God.

2 CORINTHIANS 6:14–16 NLT

If a fellow believer hurts you, go and tell him—work it out between the two of you. If he listens, you've made a friend.

MATTHEW 18:15 THE MESSAGE

Laugh with your friends when they're happy, share tears when they're down. Get along with each other; don't be stuck-up. Make friends with nobodies; don't be the great somebody.

ROMANS 12:15–16 THE MESSAGE

Become friends with God; he's already a friend with you.

2 CORINTHIANS 5:20 THE MESSAGE

— PROMISE —

Happy are those who don't listen to the wicked, who don't go where sinners go, who don't do what evil people do. They love the Lord's teachings, and they think about those teachings day and night. They are strong, like a tree planted by a river. The tree produces fruit in season, and its leaves don't die. Everything they do will succeed.

PSALM 1:1–3 NCV

My family fights all the time. Is there a way to stop the strife?

The servant of the Lord must not be quarrelsome (fighting and contending). Instead, he must be kindly to every one and mild-tempered [preserving the bond of peace].

2 TIMOTHY 2:24 AMP

Promote the kind of living that reflects wholesome teaching. . . . You yourself must be an example to them by doing good works of every kind. Let everything you do reflect the integrity and seriousness of your teaching.

TITUS 2:1, 6–8 NLT

— INSTRUCTIONS —

Always be willing to listen and slow to speak. Do not become angry easily.

JAMES 1:19 NCV

When you do things, do not let selfishness or pride be your guide. Instead, be humble and give more honor to others than to yourselves. Do not be interested only in your own life, but be interested in the lives of others.

PHILIPPIANS 2:3–4 NCV

Here is a simple, rule-of-thumb guide for behavior: Ask yourself what you want people to do for you, then grab the initiative and do it for them.

MATTHEW 7:12 THE MESSAGE

Don't use bad language. Say only what is good and helpful to those you are talking to, and what will give them a blessing.

EPHESIANS 4:29 TLB

A gentle answer will calm a person's anger, but an unkind answer will cause more anger.

PROVERBS 15:1 NCV

Get rid of all bitterness, rage and anger, brawling and slander, along with every form of malice. Be kind and compassionate to one another, forgiving each other, just as in Christ God forgave you. Be imitators of God, therefore, as dearly loved children and live a life of love.

EPHESIANS 4:31–5:2 NIV

For the whole Law is fulfilled in one word, in the statement, "You shall love your neighbor as yourself." But if you bite and devour one another, take care that you are not consumed by one another.

GALATIANS 5:14–15 NASB

What is the source of quarrels and conflicts among you? Is not the source your pleasures that wage war in your members? You lust and do not have . . .

you are envious and cannot obtain; so you fight and quarrel. You do not have because you do not ask.

James 4:1–2 NASB

Let the peace of Christ rule in your hearts.

Colossians 3:15 ESV

Do not repay evil with evil or insult with insult, but with blessing, because to this you were called so that you may inherit a blessing. . . . Who is going to harm you if you are eager to do good?

1 Peter 3:9, 13 NIV

— PROMISES —

When peacemakers plant seeds of peace, they will harvest justice.

James 3:18 CEV

When [we are] trying to please God, God makes even [our] worst enemies to be at peace with [us].

Proverbs 16:7 TLB

Turn away from evil and do good. . . . Seek peace and pursue it. The Lord confronts those who do evil.

1 Peter 3:11–12 GWT

— PRAYERS —

I pray that God will be kind to you and will let you live in perfect peace! May you keep learning more and more about God and our Lord Jesus. . . . Do your best to improve your faith. You can do this by adding goodness, understanding, self-control, patience, devotion to God, concern for others, and love. If you keep growing in this way, it will show that what you know about our Lord Jesus Christ has made your lives useful and meaningful.

2 PETER 1:2, 5–8 CEV

Now the God of peace. . . . Make you perfect in every good work to do his will, working in you that which is wellpleasing in his sight, through Jesus Christ.

HEBREWS 13:20–21 KJV

Love your enemies. Pray for those who hurt you. If you do this, you will be true children of your Father in heaven.

MATTHEW 5:44–45 NCV

— EXAMPLE —

Strife between Joseph and his brothers caused great devastation in their family:

Now as it happened, Israel loved Joseph more than any of his other children. . . . His brothers of course noticed their father's partiality, and consequently hated Joseph; they couldn't say a kind word to him.

GENESIS 37:3–4 TLB

His brothers sold Joseph as a slave, but God was with him and promoted him. Later, Joseph reconciled with his brothers, but only after he tested them to make sure their hearts had changed. (See Genesis 44:18–34.)

Then his brothers came and threw themselves down before Joseph. "Look, we are your slaves!" they said. But Joseph replied, "Don't be afraid of me. Am I God, that I can punish you? You intended to harm me, but God intended it all for good. He brought me to this position so I could save the lives of many people." . . . [Joseph] reassured them by speaking kindly to them.

GENESIS 50:18–21 NLT

Is there a way to restore a broken relationship?

In repentance and rest is your salvation, in quietness and trust is your strength.

ISAIAH 30:15 NIV

A kind answer soothes angry feelings, but harsh words stir them up.

PROVERBS 15:1 CEV

It is harder to win back the friendship of an offended brother than to capture a fortified city. His anger shuts you out like iron bars.

PROVERBS 18:19 TLB

— INSTRUCTIONS —

My dear brothers and sisters, always be willing to listen and slow to speak.

JAMES 1:19 NCV

Listen carefully to what you hear! The way you treat others will be the way you will be treated—and even worse.

MARK 4:24 CEV

Through skillful and godly Wisdom is a house (a life, a home, a family) built, and by understanding it is established [on a sound and good foundation]. And by knowledge shall the chambers [of every area] be filled with all precious and pleasant riches.

PROVERBS 24:3–4 AMP

Be happy with those who are happy, and weep with those who weep.

ROMANS 12:15 NLT

Stay away from foolish and stupid arguments, because you know they grow into quarrels. And a servant of the Lord must not quarrel but must be kind to everyone, a good teacher, and patient. The Lord's servant must gently teach those who disagree.

2 TIMOTHY 2:23–25 NCV

All of you should be of one mind. Sympathize with each other. Love each other as brothers and sisters. Be tenderhearted, and keep a humble attitude. Don't repay evil for evil. Don't retaliate with insults when people insult you. Instead, pay them back with a blessing. That is what God has called you to do, and he will bless you for it.

1 PETER 3:8–9 NLT

Be quick to listen and slow to speak or to get angry.

JAMES 1:19 CEV

Let's agree to use all our energy in getting along with each other. Help others with encouraging words; don't drag them down by finding fault.

ROMANS 14:19 THE MESSAGE

Confess your sins to each other and pray for each other so that you can live together whole and healed. The prayer of a person living right with God is something powerful to be reckoned with.

JAMES 5:16 THE MESSAGE

— PROMISES —

For I am the Lord your God, who upholds your right hand, who says to you, "Do not fear, I will help you."

ISAIAH 41:13 NASB

He will turn the hearts of the fathers to their children, and the hearts of the children to their fathers.

MALACHI 4:6 NIV

I will instruct you and teach you in the way you should go; I will counsel you and watch over you.

PSALM 32:8 NIV

Now then go, and I, even I, will be with your mouth, and teach you what you are to say.

EXODUS 4:12 NASB

— PRAYERS —

Teach me, and I will be quiet; show me where I have been wrong.

JOB 6:24 NIV

Show me your ways, O Lord, teach me your paths; guide me in your truth and teach me, for you are God my Savior, and my hope is in you all day long. . . . He guides the humble in what is right and teaches them his way.

PSALM 25:4–5, 9 NIV

— EXAMPLES —

The older brother of the Prodigal Son is a classic example of an offended person. His father listened, then quietly affirmed his love and concern:

Look, dear son, you have always stayed by me, and everything I have is yours. We had to celebrate this happy day. For your brother was dead and has come back to life! He was lost, but now he is found.

LUKE 15:31–32 NLT

When believers withdraw from Jesus, He offers His fellowship and waits patiently for the door to open:

145

Look! I stand at the door and knock. If you hear my voice and open the door, I will come in, and we will share a meal together as friends. Those who are victorious will sit with me on my throne.

REVELATION 3:20–21 NLT

My parents were critical of me—and I am sometimes critical of others. How can I break this cycle?

Let everything you say be good and helpful, so that your words will be an encouragement to those who hear them.

EPHESIANS 4:29 NLT

Be easy on people; you'll find life a lot easier.

LUKE 6:37 THE MESSAGE

— INSTRUCTIONS —

When you talk, do not say harmful things, but say what people need—words that will help others become stronger.

EPHESIANS 4:29 NCV

Be quick to listen, slow to speak, and slow to get angry. Human anger does not produce the righteousness God desires.

JAMES 1:19–20 NLT

Say only what helps, each word a gift.

EPHESIANS 4:29 THE MESSAGE

There is one who speaks rashly like the thrusts of a sword, but the tongue of the wise brings healing.

PROVERBS 12:18 NASB

Don't pick on people, jump on their failures, criticize their faults—unless, of course, you want the same treatment. That critical spirit has a way of boomeranging.

MATTHEW 7:1 THE MESSAGE

If you think you can judge others, you are wrong. When you judge them, you are really judging yourself guilty, because you do the same things they do.

ROMANS 2:1 NCV

— PROMISES —

You shall call, and the Lord will answer; you shall cry, and He will say, Here I am. If you take away from your midst yokes of oppression [wherever you find them], the finger pointed in scorn . . . and every form of false, harsh, unjust, and wicked speaking, and if you pour out that with which you sustain your own life for the hungry and satisfy the need of the afflicted, then shall your light rise in darkness and your obscurity and gloom be as the noonday. . . . And your ancient ruins shall be rebuilt; you shall raise up the foundations of . . . many generations;

and you shall be called the Repairer of the Breach, the Restorer of Streets to Dwell In.

ISAIAH 58:9–10, 12 AMP

The Lord hath given me the tongue of the learned, that I should know how to speak a word in season to him that is weary: he wakeneth morning by morning, he wakeneth mine ear to hear as the learned.

ISAIAH 50:4 KJV

— PRAYERS —

Teach me, and I will hold my tongue; cause me to understand wherein I have erred.

JOB 6:24 NKJV

I will guard my ways, lest I sin with my tongue; I will restrain my mouth with a muzzle.

PSALM 39:1 NKJV

Who can understand his errors? Cleanse me from secret faults.

PSALM 19:12 NKJV

Now may the God of peace . . . strengthen (complete, perfect) and make you what you ought to be and equip you with everything good that you may carry out His will; [while He Himself] works in you and accomplishes that which is pleasing in His sight, through Jesus Christ.

HEBREWS 13:20–21 AMP

— EXAMPLE —

Proverbs 31 gives us a profile of a virtuous woman.
When she speaks, her words build up and encourage
those around her:

She opens her mouth with wisdom, and on her tongue is
the law of kindness.

PROVERBS 31:26 NKJV

You want me to forgive them, Lord? After what they did to me?

Go ahead and be angry. You do well to be angry—but don't use your anger as fuel for revenge. And don't stay angry. Don't go to bed angry. Don't give the Devil that kind of foothold in your life. . . . Be gentle with one another, sensitive. Forgive one another as quickly and thoroughly as God in Christ forgave you.

EPHESIANS 4:26–27, 32 THE MESSAGE

— INSTRUCTIONS —

Dear friends, never avenge yourselves. Leave that to God, for he has said that he will repay those who deserve it. (Don't take the law into your own hands.) Instead, feed your enemy if he is hungry. If he is thirsty give him something to drink and you will be "heaping coals of fire on his head." In other words, he will feel ashamed of himself for what he has done to you. Don't let evil get the upper hand but conquer evil by doing good.

ROMANS 12:19–21 TLB

If you forgive men when they sin against you, your heavenly Father will also forgive you. But if you do not forgive men their sins, your Father will not forgive your sins.

MATTHEW 6:14–15 NIV

If your brother sins, rebuke him, and if he repents, forgive him. If he sins against you seven times in a day, and seven times comes back to you and says, "I repent," forgive him.

LUKE 17:3–4 NIV

Make every effort to live in peace with all men and to be holy; without holiness no one will see the Lord. See to it that no one misses the grace of God and that no bitter root grows up to cause trouble and defile many.

HEBREWS 12:14–15 NIV

Do not hate your brother in your heart.

LEVITICUS 19:17 NIV

If another believer sins against you, go privately and point out the offense. If the other person listens and confesses it, you have won that person back.

MATTHEW 18:15 NLT

Brothers, if someone is caught in a sin, you who are spiritual should restore him gently.

GALATIANS 6:1 NIV

All of you should be in agreement, understanding each other, loving each other as family, being kind and humble. Do not do wrong to repay a wrong, and do not insult to repay an insult. But repay with a blessing, because you yourselves were called to do this so that you might receive a blessing.

1 PETER 3:8–9 NCV

Judgment without mercy will be shown to anyone who has not been merciful. Mercy triumphs over judgment!

JAMES 2:13 NIV

A man's wisdom gives him patience; it is to his glory to overlook an offense.

PROVERBS 19:11 NIV

If possible, so far as it depends on you, be at peace with all men.

ROMANS 12:18 NASB

— PROMISES —

Do not judge, and you will not be judged. Do not condemn, and you will not be condemned. Forgive, and you will be forgiven.

LUKE 6:37 NIV

I can do everything through Christ, who gives me strength.

PHILIPPIANS 4:13 NLT

God blesses those people who are merciful. They will be
treated with mercy!

MATTHEW 5:7 CEV

— PRAYERS —

I pray that God will make you ready to obey him and
that you will always be eager to do right. May Jesus help
you do what pleases God.

HEBREWS 13:21 CEV

Love you enemies and pray for those who persecute you.

MATTHEW 5:44

— EXAMPLES —

*Peter asked Jesus, "Lord, how often should I forgive
someone who sins against me?" In response, Jesus told
the parable of the unforgiving servant:*

The king summoned the man and said, "You evil servant! I forgave your entire debt when you begged me
for mercy. Shouldn't you be compelled to be merciful to
your fellow servant who asked for mercy?" The king
was furious and put the screws to the man until he paid
back his entire debt. And that's exactly what my Father
in heaven is going to do to each one of you
who doesn't forgive unconditionally
anyone who asks for mercy.

MATTHEW 18:32–35 THE MESSAGE

Jesus gave us the ultimate example in forgiveness when, as He hung on the cross in terrible pain, He forgave the very ones who put Him there:

Jesus said, "Father, forgive them, for they do not know what they do."

LUKE 23:34 NKJV

My husband and I are having some problems. How can we improve our marriage?

Be agreeable, be sympathetic, be loving, be compassionate, be humble. That goes for all of you, no exceptions. No retaliation. No sharp-tongued sarcasm. Instead, bless—that's your job, to bless. You'll be a blessing and also get a blessing.

1 PETER 3:8 THE MESSAGE

Say only what is good and helpful to those you are talking to, and what will give them a blessing.

EPHESIANS 4:29 TLB

Share each other's troubles and problems.

GALATIANS 6:2 TLB

— INSTRUCTIONS —

Here is a simple, rule-of-thumb guide for behavior: Ask yourself what you want people to do for you, then grab the initiative and do it for them.

MATTHEW 7:12 THE MESSAGE

When you do things, do not let selfishness or pride be your guide. Instead, be humble and give more honor to others than to yourselves. Do not be interested only in your own life, but be interested in the lives of others.

PHILIPPIANS 2:3 NCV

Get rid of all bitterness, rage and anger, brawling and slander, along with every form of malice. Be kind and compassionate to one another, forgiving each other, just as in Christ God forgave you. Be imitators of God, therefore, as dearly loved children and live a life of love.

EPHESIANS 4:31–5:2 NIV

Out of respect for Christ, be courteously reverent to one another. Wives, understand and support your husbands in ways that show your support for Christ. The husband provides leadership to his wife the way Christ does to his church, not by domineering but by cherishing. So just as the church submits to Christ as he exercises such leadership, wives should likewise submit to their husbands. Husbands, go all out in your love for your wives, exactly as Christ did for the church—a love marked by giving, not getting. Christ's love makes the church whole. His words evoke her beauty. Everything he does and says is designed to bring the best out of her, dressing her in dazzling white silk, radiant with holiness. And that is how husbands ought to love their wives. They're really doing themselves a favor— since they're already "one" in marriage.

EPHESIANS 5:21–28 THE MESSAGE

Honor Christ by submitting to each other.

EPHESIANS 5:21 TLB

Wives, yield to the authority of your husbands, because this is the right thing to do in the Lord. Husbands, love your wives and be gentle with them.

COLOSSIANS 3:18–19 NCV

Be good wives to your husbands, responsive to their needs. There are husbands who, indifferent as they are to any words about God, will be captivated by your life of holy beauty. What matters is not your outer appearance—the styling of your hair, the jewelry you wear, the cut of your clothes—but your inner disposition. Cultivate inner beauty, the gentle, gracious kind that God delights in. . . .The same goes for you husbands: Be good husbands to your wives. Honor them, delight in them. As women they lack some of your advantages. But in the new life of God's grace, you're equals. Treat your wives, then, as equals so your prayers don't run aground.

1 PETER 3:1–4, 7 THE MESSAGE

Don't pick on people, jump on their failures, criticize their faults—unless, of course, you want the same treatment. That critical spirit has a way of boomeranging. It's easy to see a smudge on your neighbor's face and be oblivious to the ugly sneer on your own. Do you have the nerve to say, "Let me wash your face for you," when your own face is distorted by contempt? . . .

Wipe that ugly sneer off your own face, and you might be fit to offer a washcloth to your neighbor.

MATTHEW 7:1–5 THE MESSAGE

Give away your life; you'll find life given back, but not merely given back—given back with bonus and blessing. Giving, not getting, is the way. Generosity begets generosity.

LUKE 6:37–38 THE MESSAGE

If you give, you will get! Your gift will return to you in full and overflowing measure, pressed down, shaken together to make room for more, and running over. Whatever measure you use to give—large or small— will be used to measure what is given back to you.

LUKE 6:38 TLB

For the whole law can be summed up in this one command: "Love your neighbor as yourself." But if you are always biting and devouring one another, watch out! Beware of destroying one another.

GALATIANS 5:14–15 NLT

It is obvious what kind of life develops out of trying to get your own way all the time: repetitive, loveless, cheap sex; a stinking accumulation of mental and emotional garbage; frenzied and joyless grabs for happiness; trinket gods; magic-show religion; paranoid loneliness; cutthroat competition; all-consuming-yet-never-satisfied wants; a brutal temper; an impotence to love or be loved; divided homes and divided lives; small-minded and lopsided pursuits; the vicious habit of depersonalizing everyone into a rival; uncontrolled and uncontrollable addictions; ugly parodies of community. I could go on. This isn't the first time I have warned you, you know. If you use your freedom this way, you will not inherit God's kingdom.

GALATIANS 5:19–21 THE MESSAGE

Where do you think all these appalling wars and quarrels come from? Do you think they just happen? Think again. They come about because you want your own way, and fight for it deep inside yourselves. You lust for what you don't have and are willing to kill to get it. You want what isn't yours and will risk violence to get your hands on it. You wouldn't think of just asking God for it, would you? And why not? Because you know you'd be asking for what you have no right to. You're spoiled children, each wanting your own way.

JAMES 4:1–3 THE MESSAGE

In your anger do not sin: Do not let the sun go down while you are still angry, and do not give the devil a foothold.

EPHESIANS 4:26–27 NIV

A man's discretion makes him slow to anger, and it is his glory to overlook a transgression.

PROVERBS 19:11 NASB

Keeping away from strife is an honor for a man, but any fool will quarrel. . . . A plan in the heart of a man is like deep water, but a man of understanding draws it out.

PROVERBS 20:3, 5 NASB

Make this your common practice: Confess your sins to each other and pray for each other so that you can live together whole and healed. The prayer of a person living right with God is something powerful to be reckoned with.

JAMES 5:16 THE MESSAGE

Do the hard work of getting along with each other, treating each other with dignity and honor.

JAMES 3:18 THE MESSAGE

Let the peace of Christ keep you in tune with each other, in step with each other. None of this going off and doing your own thing. And cultivate thankfulness.

COLOSSIANS 3:15 THE MESSAGE

If ye have bitter envying and strife in your hearts, glory not, and lie not against the truth. This wisdom descendeth not from above, but is earthly, sensual, devilish. For where envying and strife is, there is confusion and every evil work.

JAMES 3:14–16 KJV

Those who are peacemakers will plant seeds of peace and reap a harvest of righteousness.

JAMES 3:18 NLT

Lord, you establish peace for us; all that we have accomplished you have done for us.

ISAIAH 26:12 NIV

For he himself is our peace, who has made the two one and has destroyed the barrier, the dividing wall of hostility.

EPHESIANS 2:14 NIV

[Not in your own strength] for it is God Who is all the while effectually at work in you [energizing and creating in you the power and desire], both to will and to work for His good pleasure and satisfaction and delight.

PHILIPPIANS 2:13 AMP

God can do anything, you know—far more than you could ever imagine or guess or request in your wildest dreams! He does it not by pushing us around but by working within us, his Spirit deeply and gently within us.

EPHESIANS 3:20 THE MESSAGE

If you want to enjoy life and see many happy days, keep your tongue from speaking evil and keep your lips from telling lies. Turn away from evil and do good. Search for peace, and work to maintain it. The eyes of the Lord watch over those who do right, and his ears are open to their prayers. But the Lord turns his face against those who do evil.

1 PETER 3:10–12 NLT

No temptation has overtaken you except such as is common to man; but God is faithful, who will not allow you to be tempted beyond what you are able, but with the temptation will also make the way of escape, that you may be able to bear it.

1 CORINTHIANS 10:13 NKJV

The Lord knows how to rescue godly people from their trials.

2 PETER 2:9 NLT

— PRAYERS —

We pray that you'll have the strength to stick it out over the long haul—not the grim strength of gritting your teeth but the glory-strength God gives. It is strength that endures the unendurable and spills over into joy.

COLOSSIANS 1:11 THE MESSAGE

Now the God of peace . . . make you perfect in every good work to do his will, working in you that which is wellpleasing in his sight, through Jesus Christ.

HEBREWS 13:20-21 KJV

With this in mind, we constantly pray for you . . . that by his power he may fulfill every good purpose of yours and every act prompted by your faith.

2 THESSALONIANS 1:11 NIV

We pray for you all the time—pray that our God will make you fit for what he's called you to be, pray that he'll fill your good ideas and acts of faith with his own energy so that it all amounts to something.

2 THESSALONIANS 1:11 THE MESSAGE

— EXAMPLES —

David and Bathsheba's relationship got off to a bad start: adultery, deception, even murder. Yet with God's forgiveness, grace, and help, they overcame their problems, and God used their union to bless all the nations of the earth:

A record of the genealogy of Jesus Christ the son of David, the son of Abraham: Abraham was the father of Isaac, Isaac the father of Jacob, Jacob the father of Judah and his brothers . . . Jesse the father of King David. David was the father of Solomon, whose mother had been Uriah's wife.

MATTHEW 1:1–2, 6 NIV

Solomon tells how David and Bathsheba worked together to teach him God's wisdom:

When I was a boy in my father's house, still tender, and an only child of my mother, he taught me and said, "Lay hold of my words with all your heart; keep my commands and you will live."

PROVERBS 4:3–4 NIV

My child, listen when your father corrects you. Don't neglect your mother's instruction. What you learn from them will crown you with grace and be a chain of honor around your neck.

PROVERBS 1:8–9 NLT

Lord, do I have to wait until you choose a mate for me?

Fathers can give their sons an inheritance of houses and wealth, but only the Lord can give an understanding wife.

PROVERBS 19:14 NLT

The man who finds a wife finds a good thing; she is a blessing to him from the Lord.

PROVERBS 18:22 TLB

— INSTRUCTIONS —

And the Lord God said, "It isn't good for man to be alone; I will make a companion for him, a helper suited to his needs."

GENESIS 2:18 TLB

Every good thing given and every perfect gift is from above, coming down from the Father of lights.

JAMES 1:17 NASB

Your heavenly Father will give good things to those who ask him!

MATTHEW 7:11 NCV

Remember, your Father knows exactly what you need even before you ask him!

MATTHEW 6:8 TLB

In his heart a man plans his course, but the Lord determines his steps.

PROVERBS 16:9 NIV

We humans keep brainstorming options and plans, but God's purpose prevails.

PROVERBS 19:21 THE MESSAGE

You're blessed when you stay on course, walking steadily on the road revealed by God. You're blessed when you follow his directions, doing your best to find him. That's right—you don't go off on your own; you walk straight along the road he set.

PSALM 119:1–3 THE MESSAGE

— PROMISES —

The Lord will guide you continually, and satisfy you with all good things.

ISAIAH 58:11 TLB

Delight yourself in the Lord; and He will give you the desires of your heart.

PSALM 37:4 NASB

He is close to all who call on him sincerely. He fulfills the desires of those who reverence and trust him; he hears their cries for help and rescues them.

PSALM 145:18–19 TLB

The Lord gives grace and glory; no good thing does He withhold from those who walk uprightly.

PSALM 84:11 NASB

— PRAYER —

May he give you the desire of your heart and make all your plans succeed.

PSALM 20:4 NIV

There is someone I care about who needs to know you, Lord. What can I do?

Everywhere we go we talk about Christ to all who will listen, warning them and teaching them as well as we know how. We want to be able to present each one to God, perfect because of what Christ has done for each of them.

COLOSSIANS 1:28 TLB

— INSTRUCTIONS —

If anybody asks why you believe as you do, be ready to tell him.

1 PETER 3:15 TLB

When you are with unbelievers, always make good use of the time. Be pleasant and hold their interest when you speak the message. Choose your words carefully and be ready to give answers to anyone who asks questions.

COLOSSIANS 4:5–6 CEV

Such confidence as this is ours through Christ before God. Not that we are competent in ourselves . . . but our competence comes from God. He has made us competent as ministers of a new covenant.

2 CORINTHIANS 3:4–6 NIV

I urge, then, first of all, that requests, prayers, intercession and thanksgiving be made for everyone. . . . This is good, and pleases God our Savior, who wants all men to be saved and to come to a knowledge of the truth.

1 TIMOTHY 2:1, 3–4 NIV

Open their eyes so that they may turn from darkness to light and from the dominion of Satan to God, that they may receive forgiveness of sins and an inheritance among those who have been sanctified by faith in Me.

ACTS 26:18 NASB

Now this is the confidence that we have in Him, that if we ask anything according to His will, He hears us. And if we know that He hears us, whatever we ask, we know that we have the petitions that we have asked of Him.

1 JOHN 5:14–15 NKJV

Behold, I have given you authority to tread on serpents and scorpions, and over all the power of the enemy, and nothing will injure you.

LUKE 10:19 NASB

And I will give you the keys of the kingdom of heaven, and whatever you bind on earth will be bound in heaven, and whatever you loose on earth will be loosed in heaven.

MATTHEW 16:19 NKJV

— PROMISES —

I was found by those who did not seek me; I revealed myself to those who did not ask for me.

ROMANS 10:20 NIV

For thus says the Lord God, "Behold, I Myself will search for My sheep and seek them out. . . . I will seek the lost, bring back the scattered, bind up the broken and strengthen the sick."

EZEKIEL 34:11, 16 NASB

I will lead the blind by ways they have not known, along unfamiliar paths I will guide them; I will turn the darkness into light before them and make the rough places smooth. These are the things I will do; I will not forsake them.

ISAIAH 42:16 NIV

Those who err in spirit will come to understanding, and those who murmur [discontentedly] will accept instruction.

ISAIAH 29:24 AMP

Thus says the Lord, "In an acceptable and favorable time I have heard and answered you, and in a day of salvation I have helped you. . . . saying to those who are bound, 'Come forth,' and to those who are in [spiritual] darkness, 'Show yourselves [come into the light].' "

ISAIAH 49:8–9 AMP

— TO PRAY FOR THE LOST ONE —

I . . . do not cease giving thanks for you, while making mention of you in my prayers; that the God of our Lord Jesus Christ, the Father of glory, may give to you a spirit of wisdom and of revelation in the knowledge of Him. I pray that the eyes of your heart may be enlightened, so that you will know what is the hope of His calling, what are the riches of the glory of His inheritance in the saints, and what is the surpassing greatness of His power toward us who believe.

EPHESIANS 1:15–19 NASB

My response is to get down on my knees before the Father. . . . I ask him to strengthen you by his Spirit— not a brute strength but a glorious inner strength—that Christ will live in you as you open the door and invite him in.

EPHESIANS 3:14, 16–17 THE MESSAGE

We ask God to give you complete knowledge of his will and to give you spiritual wisdom and understanding.

COLOSSIANS 1:9 NLT

And may the God of peace Himself sanctify you through and through [separate you from profane things, make you pure and wholly consecrated to God]; and may your spirit and soul and body be preserved sound and complete [and found] blameless at the coming of our Lord Jesus Christ (the Messiah). Faithful is He Who is calling you [to Himself] and utterly trustworthy, and He will also do it [that is, fulfill His call by hallowing and keeping you].

1 THESSALONIANS 5:23–24 AMP

I WANT TO BE
A BETTER
PARENT

God, what kind of parent do you want me to be? What can I do for my children?

Be imitators of God [copy Him and follow His example] as well-beloved children [imitate their father]. And walk in love [esteeming and delighting in one another] as Christ loved us and gave Himself up for us.

EPHESIANS 5:1–2 AMP

— INSTRUCTIONS —

Above all, love each other deeply, because love covers over a multitude of sins.

1 PETER 4:8 NIV

Let love be your guide. Christ loved us and offered his life for us as a sacrifice that pleases God.

EPHESIANS 5:2 CEV

Put on a heart of compassion, kindness, humility, gentleness and patience; bearing with one another, and forgiving each other, whoever has a complaint against any one; just as the Lord forgave you, so also should you.

Beyond all these things put on love, which is the perfect bond of unity.

COLOSSIANS 3:12–14 NASB

Carry each other's burdens, and in this way you will fulfill the law of Christ.

GALATIANS 6:2 NIV

Let the Word of Christ—the Message—have the run of the house. Give it plenty of room in your lives. Instruct and direct one another using good common sense. And sing, sing your hearts out to God! Let every detail in your lives—words, actions, whatever—be done in the name of the Master, Jesus, thanking God the Father every step of the way.

COLOSSIANS 3:16–17 THE MESSAGE

Correct your son, and he will give you comfort; he will also delight your soul.

PROVERBS 29:17 NASB

Train up a child in the way he should go, even when he is old he will not depart from it.

PROVERBS 22:6 NASB

Fathers, do not irritate and provoke your children to anger [do not exasperate them to resentment], but rear them [tenderly] in the training and discipline and the counsel and admonition of the Lord.

EPHESIANS 6:4 AMP

I will teach you hidden lessons from our past—stories we have heard and known, stories our ancestors handed down to us. We will not hide these truths from our children; we will tell the next generation about the glorious deeds of the Lord, about his power and his mighty wonders. . . . So each generation should set its hope anew on God, not forgetting his glorious miracles and obeying his commands.

PSALM 78:2–4, 7 NLT

Do not be bitter or angry or mad. Never shout angrily or say things to hurt others. Never do anything evil.

EPHESIANS 4:31 NCV

Fathers, do not . . . irritate . . . your children [do not be hard on them or harass them], lest they become discouraged and sullen and morose and feel inferior and frustrated. [Do not break their spirit.]

COLOSSIANS 3:21 AMP

Fathers . . . take them by the hand and lead them in the way of the Master.

EPHESIANS 6:4 THE MESSAGE

As a father loves and pities his children, so the Lord loves and pities those who fear Him [with reverence, worship and awe]. For He knows our frame; He [earnestly] remembers and imprints [on his heart] that we are dust.

PSALM 103:13–14 AMP

Gently encourage the stragglers, and reach out for the exhausted, pulling them to their feet. Be patient with each person, attentive to individual needs. And be careful that when you get on each other's nerves you don't snap at each other. Look for the best in each other, and always do your best to bring it out.

1 THESSALONIANS 5:14–15 THE MESSAGE

With each of you we were like a father with his child, holding your hand, whispering encouragement, showing you step-by-step how to live well before God, who called us into his own kingdom, into this delightful life.

1 THESSALONIANS 2:11–12 THE MESSAGE

As for me and my house, we will serve the Lord.

JOSHUA 24:15 NASB

— PRAYERS —

Pray at all times (on every occasion, in every season) in the Spirit, with all [manner of] prayer and entreaty.

EPHESIANS 6:18 AMP

May the God of peace . . . equip you with everything good for doing his will, and may he work in us what is pleasing to him, through Jesus Christ, to whom be glory for ever and ever. Amen.

HEBREWS 13:20–21 NIV

What is God's purpose for my family?

He seeks godly offspring.

MALACHI 2:15 NKJV

Now the Lord said to Abram, "Go forth from your country, and from your relatives and from your father's house, to the land which I will show you; and I will make you a great nation, and I will bless you. . . . And in you all the families of the earth shall be blessed."

GENESIS 12:1–3 NASB

All the ends of the earth will remember and turn to the Lord, and all the families of the nations will worship before You. For the kingdom is the Lord's and He rules over the nations.

PSALM 22:27–28 NASB

After these things I looked, and behold, a great multitude which no one could count, from every nation and all tribes and peoples and tongues, standing before the throne and before the Lamb, clothed in white robes, and palm branches were in their hands.

REVELATION 7:9 NASB

— PROMISES —

They will be my people, and I will be their God. And I will give them one heart and one purpose: to worship me forever, for their own good and for the good of all their descendants. And I will make an everlasting covenant with them: I will never stop doing good for them.

JEREMIAH 32:38–40 NLT

Behold, children are a gift of the Lord, the fruit of the womb is a reward.

PSALM 127:3 NASB

Like a warrior's fistful of arrows are the children of a vigorous youth. Oh, how blessed are you parents, with your quivers full of children!

PSALM 127:4–5 THE MESSAGE

Children's children are a crown to the aged, and parents are the pride of their children.

PROVERBS 17:6 NIV

The father of godly children has cause for joy. What a pleasure it is to have children who are wise.

PROVERBS 23:24 NLT

Correct your son, and he will give you rest; Yes, he will give delight to your soul.

PROVERBS 29:17 NKJV

— EXAMPLE —

God chose Abraham to be His covenant partner because He trusted Abraham to discipline his children and teach them to do right. Abraham gave the Lord godly offspring through which He could then bless all the nations of the earth:

For I know him, that he will command his children and his household after him, and they shall keep the way of the Lord, to do justice and judgment; that the Lord may bring upon Abraham that which he hath spoken of him.

GENESIS 18:19 KJV

Lord, how should I pray for my children?

This is what I want you to do: Ask the Father for whatever is in keeping with the things I've revealed to you. Ask in my name, according to my will, and he'll most certainly give it to you.

JOHN 16:23–24 THE MESSAGE

Rise during the night and cry out. Pour out your hearts like water to the Lord. Lift up your hands to him in prayer, pleading for your children.

LAMENTATIONS 2:19 NLT

— INSTRUCTIONS —

Keep on asking, and you will receive what you ask for. Keep on seeking, and you will find. Keep on knocking, and the door will be opened to you. For everyone who asks, receives. Everyone who seeks, finds. And to everyone who knocks, the door will be opened. You parents—if your children ask for a loaf of bread, do you give them a stone instead? Or if they ask for a fish, do you give them a snake? Of course not! So if you sinful people know how to give good gifts to your children, how

how much more will your heavenly Father give good gifts to those who ask him.

MATTHEW 7:7–11 NLT

I am the vine, and you are the branches. If you stay joined to me, and I stay joined to you, then you will produce lots of fruit. But you cannot do anything without me. . . . Stay joined to me and let my teachings become part of you. Then you can pray for whatever you want, and your prayer will be answered.

JOHN 15:5, 7 CEV

God is strong, and he wants you strong. So take everything the Master has set out for you, well-made weapons of the best materials. And put them to use so you will be able to stand up to everything the Devil throws your way. This is no afternoon athletic contest that we'll walk away from and forget about in a couple of hours. This is for keeps, a life-or-death fight to the finish against the Devil and all his angels.

Be prepared. You're up against far more than you can handle on your own. Take all the help you can get, every weapon God has issued, so that when it's all over but the shouting you'll still be on your feet. . . . God's Word is an indispensable weapon. In the same way, prayer is essential in this ongoing warfare. Pray hard and long.

EPHESIANS 6:10–18 THE MESSAGE

Never give up praying. And when you pray, keep alert and be thankful.

COLOSSIANS 4:2 CEV

Always pray by the power of the Spirit.

EPHESIANS 6:18 CEV

The Holy Spirit helps us in our weakness. For example, we don't know what God wants us to pray for. But the Holy Spirit prays for us with groanings that cannot be expressed in words. And the Father who knows all hearts knows what the Spirit is saying, for the Spirit pleads for us believers in harmony with God's own will.

ROMANS 8:26–27 NLT

I will pray with the spirit, and I will also pray with the understanding.

1 CORINTHIANS 14:15 NKJV

— PROMISES —

Then said the Lord to me . . . I am alert and active, watching over My word to perform it.

JEREMIAH 1:12 AMP

This is the confidence which we have before Him, that, if we ask anything according to His will, He hears us. And if we know that He hears us in whatever we ask, we know that we have the requests which we have asked from Him.

1 JOHN 5:14–15 NASB

"Have faith in God," Jesus answered. "I tell you the truth, if anyone says to this mountain, 'Go, throw yourself

into the sea,' and does not doubt in his heart but believes
that what he says will happen, it will be done for him.
Therefore, I tell you, whatever you ask for in prayer,
believe that you have received it, and it will be yours."

MARK 11:22–24 NIV

Let us then fearlessly and confidently and boldly draw
near to the throne of grace . . . that we may receive
mercy . . . and find grace to help in good time for every
need [appropriate help and well-timed help, coming just
when we need it].

HEBREWS 4:16 AMP

The earnest (heartfelt, continued) prayer of a righteous
man makes tremendous power available [dynamic in its
working].

JAMES 5:16 AMP

With God's power working in us, God can do much,
much more than anything we can ask or imagine.

EPHESIANS 3:20 NCV

— TO PRAY FOR YOUR CHILD —

I pray that Christ will live in your hearts by faith and
that your life will be strong in love and be built on love.
And I pray that you . . . will have the power to understand the greatness of Christ's love—how wide and how
long and how high and how deep that love is. Christ's
love is greater than anyone can ever know, but I pray

that you will be able to know that love. Then you can be filled with the fullness of God.

EPHESIANS 3:17–19 NCV

We ask God to give you a complete knowledge of his will and to give you spiritual wisdom and understanding. Then the way you live will always honor and please the Lord, and your lives will produce every kind of good fruit. All the while you will grow as you learn to know God better and better. We also pray that you will be strengthened with all his glorious power so you will have all the endurance and patience you need. May you be filled with joy, always thanking the Father.

COLOSSIANS 1:9–12 NLT

Father . . . keep them safe from the evil one.

JOHN 17:15 CEV

— EXAMPLE —

Manoah, Samson's father, prayed for wisdom on how to raise his son:

Lord, please let the man of God come back to us again and give us more instructions about this son who is to be born. . . . When your words come true, what kind of rules should govern the boy's life and work?

JUDGES 13:8, 12 NLT

How can I be more loving to my family?

Watch what God does, and then you do it, like children who learn proper behavior from their parents. Mostly what God does is love you. Keep company with him and learn a life of love. Observe how Christ loved us. His love was not cautious but extravagant. He didn't love in order to get something from us but to give everything of himself to us. Love like that.

Ephesians 5:1–2 the message

— INSTRUCTIONS —

You must quit being angry, hateful, and evil. You must no longer say insulting or cruel things about others. And stop lying to each other. You have given up your old way of life with its habits. Each of you is now a new person. You are becoming more and more like your Creator. . . . So be gentle, kind, humble, meek, and patient. Put up with each other, and forgive anyone who does you wrong, just as Christ has forgiven you.

Colossians 3:8–10, 12–13 cev

Above all things have fervent love for one another, for "love will cover a multitude of sins."

1 Peter 4:8 nkjv

All who confess that Jesus is the Son of God have God living in them, and they live in God. . . . As we live in God, our love grows more perfect. . . . We love each other because he loved us first.

1 JOHN 4:15, 17, 19 NLT

Give as freely as you have received!
MATTHEW 10:8 NLT

Love endures long and is patient and kind; love never is envious nor boils over with jealousy, is not boastful or vainglorious, does not display itself haughtily. It is not conceited (arrogant and inflated with pride); it is not rude (unmannerly), and does not act unbecomingly.

Love (God's love in us) does not insist on its own rights or its own way, for it is not self-seeking; it is not touchy or fretful or resentful; it takes no account of the evil done to it [it pays no attention to a suffered wrong]. It does not rejoice at injustice and unrighteousness, but rejoices when right and truth prevail. Love bears up under anything and everything that comes, is ever ready to believe the best of every person, its hopes are fadeless under all circumstances and it endures everything [without weakening]. Love never fails [never fades out or becomes obsolete or comes to an end].

1 CORINTHIANS 13:4–8 AMP

— PROMISES —

But the Holy Spirit produces this kind of fruit in our lives: love, joy, peace, patience, kindness, goodness, faithfulness, gentleness, and self-control.

GALATIANS 5:22–23 NLT

God has poured out his love into our hearts by the Holy Spirit, whom he has given us.

ROMANS 5:5 NIV

God is not unjust; he will not forget your work and the love you have shown him as you have helped his people and continue to help them.

HEBREWS 6:10 NIV

— PRAYERS —

May the Lord make your love increase and overflow for each other and for everyone else, just as ours does for you.

1 THESSALONIANS 3:12 NIV

I pray that the Lord will guide you to be as loving as God and as patient as Christ.

2 THESSALONIANS 3:5 CEV

We pray that our Lord Jesus Christ and God our Father will encourage you and help you always to do and say the right thing.

2 THESSALONIANS 2:16–17 CEV

Your roots will grow down into God's love and keep you strong. And may you have the power to understand . . . how wide, how long, how high, and how deep his love is. May you experience the love of Christ, though it is too great to understand it fully. Then you will be made complete with all the fullness of life and power that comes from God.

EPHESIANS 3:17–19 NLT

We also pray that you will be strengthened with his glorious power so that you will have all the patience and endurance you need.

COLOSSIANS 1:11 NLT

I pray that your love will overflow more and more, and that you will keep on growing in your knowledge and understanding. For I want you to understand what really matters, so that you may live pure and blameless lives until the day of Christ's return. May you always be filled with the fruit of your salvation—the righteous character produced in your life by Jesus Christ—for this will bring much glory and praise to God.

PHILIPPIANS 1:9–11 NLT

— EXAMPLE —

God gave us the ultimate example of love:

This is how God showed his love for us: God sent his only Son into the world so we might live through him. . . . If God loved us like this, we certainly ought to love each other.

1 JOHN 4:9, 11 THE MESSAGE

If we love each other, God lives in us, and his love is brought to full expression in us.

1 JOHN 4:12 NLT

Good fathers give consistent discipline. How can I get better at this?

Discipline your children; you'll be glad you did—they'll turn out delightful to live with.

PROVERBS 29:17 THE MESSAGE

A refusal to correct is a refusal to love; love your children by disciplining them.

PROVERBS 13:24 THE MESSAGE

— INSTRUCTIONS —

Teach a child to choose the right path, and when he is older he will remain upon it.

PROVERBS 22:6 TLB

Fathers, do not provoke your children to anger, but bring them up in the discipline and instruction of the Lord.

EPHESIANS 6:4 NASB

All Scripture is inspired by God and is useful for teaching, for showing people what is wrong in their lives, for correcting faults, and for teaching how to live right. Using the Scriptures, the person who serves God will be capable, having all that is needed to do every good work.

2 TIMOTHY 3:16–17 NCV

Fathers, don't exasperate your children by coming down hard on them. Take them by the hand and lead them in the way of the Master.

EPHESIANS 6:4 THE MESSAGE

Don't fail to discipline your children. They won't die if you spank them. Physical discipline may well save them from death.

PROVERBS 23:13–14 NLT

Foolishness is bound up in the heart of a child; the rod of correction will drive it far from him.

PROVERBS 22:15 NKJV

The rod of correction imparts wisdom, but a child left to himself disgraces his mother.

PROVERBS 29:15 NIV

— INSTRUCTIONS FOR YOUR CHILD —

You are living a brand new kind of life that is continually learning more and more of what is right, and trying constantly to be more and more like Christ who created this new life within you. . . . Remember what Christ taught and let his words enrich your lives and make you wise.

COLOSSIANS 3:10, 16 TLB

Since you were a child you have known the Holy Scriptures which are able to make you wise. And that wisdom leads to salvation through faith in Christ Jesus.

2 TIMOTHY 3:15 NCV

My children, listen to your father's teaching. Pay attention so you will understand. . . . Do not forget what I teach you. I was once a young boy in my father's house. I was like an only child to my mother. And my father taught me and said, "Hold on to my words with all your heart. Keep my commands and you will live. Get wisdom and understanding. Don't forget or ignore my words. Use wisdom, and it will take care of you. Love wisdom, and it will keep you safe. Wisdom is the most important thing. So get wisdom. If it costs everything you have, get understanding.

PROVERBS 4:1–7 ICB

It is never fun to be corrected. In fact, at the time it is always painful. But if we learn to obey by being corrected, we will do right and live at peace.

HEBREWS 12:11 CEV

A person who refuses correction will end up poor and disgraced. But a person who accepts correction will be honored.

PROVERBS 13:18 ICB

Only a fool despises a parent's discipline; whoever learns from correction is wise.

PROVERBS 15:5 NLT

Children, obey your parents; this is the right thing to do because God has placed them in authority over you. Honor your father and mother. This is the first of God's Ten Commandments that ends with a promise. And this is the promise: that if you honor your father and mother, yours will be a long life, full of blessing.

EPHESIANS 6:1–3 TLB

— EXAMPLE —

God, the ultimate Father, disciplines His children with love, patience, and consistency:

My child, don't think the Lord's discipline is worth nothing, and don't stop trying when he corrects you. The Lord disciplines those he loves, and he punishes everyone he accepts as his child.

So hold on through your sufferings, because they are like a father's discipline. God is treating you as children. All children are disciplined by their fathers. If you are never disciplined (and every child must be disciplined), you are not true children. . . .

Our fathers on earth disciplined us for a short time in the way they thought was best. But God disciplines us to help us, so we can become holy as he is. We do not enjoy being disciplined. It is painful, but later, after we have learned from it, we have peace, because we start living in the right way.

HEBREWS 12:5–8, 10–11 NCV

Lord, I worry about my children's safety. Will you protect them?

If you respect the Lord, you and your children have a strong fortress and a life-giving fountain that keeps you safe from deadly traps.

PROVERBS 14:26–27 CEV

Those who know Your name will put their trust in You; for You, Lord, have not forsaken those who seek You.

PSALM 9:10 NKJV

— INSTRUCTIONS —

Don't worry about anything; instead, pray about everything. Tell God what you need, and thank him for all he has done. Then you will experience God's peace, which exceeds anything we can understand. His peace will guard your hearts and minds as you live in Christ Jesus. One final thing. Fix your thoughts on what is true, and honorable, and right, and pure, and lovely, and admirable. Think about things that are excellent and worthy of praise.

PHILIPPIANS 4:6–8 NLT

Give your burdens to the Lord, and He will take care of you. He will not permit the godly to slip and fall.

PSALM 55:22 NLT

Give all your worries and cares to God, for He cares about you.

1 PETER 5:7 NLT

— PROMISES —

I am leaving you with a gift—peace of mind and heart. And the peace I give is a gift the world cannot give. So don't be troubled or afraid.

JOHN 14:27 NLT

The Lord is my light and my salvation—so why should I be afraid? The Lord is my fortress, protecting me from danger, so why should I tremble?

PSALM 27:1 NLT

In righteousness you shall be established; you shall be far from oppression, for you shall not fear; and from terror, for it shall not come near you.

ISAIAH 54:14 NKJV

Those who live in the shelter of the Most High will find rest in the shadow of the Almighty. This I declare of the Lord: He alone is my refuge, my place of safety; he is my God, and I trust him.

PSALM 91:1–2 NLT

You are my hiding place; you will protect me from trouble and surround me with songs of deliverance.

PSALM 32:7 NIV

— PROMISES FOR YOUR CHILD —

He will rescue you from every trap and protect you from deadly disease. He will cover you with his feathers. He will shelter you with his wings. His faithful promises are your armor and protection. Do not be afraid of the terrors of the night, nor the arrow that flies in the day. . . . Though a thousand fall at your side, though ten thousand are dying around you, these evils will not touch you. . . . For he will order his angels to protect you wherever you go.

PSALM 91:3–5, 7, 11 NLT

The Lord says, "I will rescue those who love me. I will protect those who trust in my name. When they call on me, I will answer; I will be with them in trouble. I will rescue and honor them. I will reward them with a long life and give them my salvation."

PSALM 91:14–16 NLT

But the Lord is faithful, and he will strengthen and protect you from the evil one.

2 THESSALONIANS 3:3 NIV

The angel of the Lord encamps around those who fear Him, and rescues them.

PSALM 34:7 NASB

— PRAYERS —

May the God of hope fill you with all joy and peace as
you trust in him, so that you may overflow with hope by
the power of the Holy Spirit.

ROMANS 15:13 NIV

In the multitude of my [anxious] thoughts within me,
Your comforts cheer and delight my soul!

PSALM 94:19 AMP

— EXAMPLE —

*Pharaoh hardened his heart and refused to let the
children of Israel go free. Moses warned him: "Every
firstborn son in Egypt will die" (Exodus 11:5 NIV). But
Pharaoh did not heed the warning:*

Then Moses summoned all the elders of Israel and said
to them, "Go at once and . . . slaughter the Passover
lamb. Take a bunch of hyssop, dip it into the blood in the
basin and put some of the blood on the top and on both
sides of the doorframe. Not one of you shall go out the
door of his house until morning. When the Lord goes
through the land . . . he will see the blood . . . and will
pass over that doorway, and he will not permit
the destroyer to enter your houses and strike
you down."

EXODUS 12:21–23 NIV

There was a death in every Egyptian house. But among God's people, every child was protected because of the faith and obedience of his parents.

How can I communicate—
heart to heart—
with my child?

My dear brothers and sisters, always be willing to listen
and slow to speak.

JAMES 1:19 NCV

— INSTRUCTIONS —

Listen carefully to what you hear! The way you treat
others will be the way you will be treated.

MARK 4:24 CEV

Be happy with those who are happy, and weep with
those who weep.

ROMANS 12:15 NLT

The purposes of a man's heart are deep waters, but a
man of understanding draws them out.

PROVERBS 20:5 NIV

The heart of the discerning acquires knowledge; the ears
of the wise seek it out.

PROVERBS 18:15 NIV

Let the wise listen and add to their learning.

PROVERBS 1:5 NIV

— PROMISE —

Through skillful and godly Wisdom is a house (a life, a home, a family) built, and by understanding it is established [on a sound and good foundation], and by knowledge shall the chambers [of its every area] be filled with all precious and pleasant riches.

PROVERBS 24:3–4 AMP

— EXAMPLE —

Time spent with children is never wasted:

Jesus called a little child to him. . . . Then he said . . . "I tell you the truth, you must change and become like little children. Otherwise, you will never enter the kingdom of heaven. The greatest person in the kingdom of heaven is the one who makes himself humble like this child. Whoever accepts a child in my name accepts me."

MATTHEW 18:2–5 NCV

My child is withdrawing from me. How can I restore our close relationship?

In repentance and rest is your salvation, in quietness and trust is your strength.

ISAIAH 30:15 NIV

A kind answer soothes angry feelings, but harsh words stir them up.

PROVERBS 15:1 CEV

— INSTRUCTIONS —

Stay away from foolish and stupid arguments, because you know they grow into quarrels. And a servant of the Lord must not quarrel but must be kind to everyone, a good teacher, and patient. The Lord's servant must gently teach those who disagree.

2 TIMOTHY 2:23–25 NCV

All of you should be of one mind. Sympathize with one another. Love each other as brothers and sisters. Be tenderhearted and keep a humble attitude. Don't repay evil for evil. Don't retaliate with insults when people insult you. Instead, pay them back with a blessing. That is what God has called you to do, and he will bless you for it.

1 PETER 3:8–9 NLT

Be quick to listen and slow to speak or to get angry.

JAMES 1:19 CEV

Let's agree to use all our energy in getting along with each other. Help others with encouraging words; don't drag them down by finding fault.

ROMANS 14:19 THE MESSAGE

Rejoice with those who rejoice; mourn with those who mourn. Live in harmony with one another.

ROMANS 12:15–16 NIV

Confess your sins to each other and pray for each other so that you can live together whole and healed. The prayer of a person living right with God is something powerful to be reckoned with.

JAMES 5:16 THE MESSAGE

He who covers his transgressions will not prosper, but whoever confesses and forsakes his sins shall obtain mercy.

PROVERBS 28:13 AMP

— PROMISES —

I am the Lord your God, who upholds your right hand,
who says to you, "Do not fear, I will help you."

ISAIAH 41:13 NASB

He will turn the hearts of the fathers to their children,
and the hearts of the children to their fathers.

MALACHI 4:6 NIV

I will instruct you and teach you in the way you should
go; I will counsel you and watch over you.

PSALM 32:8 NIV

Now then go, and I, even I, will be with your mouth, and
teach you what you are to say.

EXODUS 4:12 NASB

— PRAYERS —

Teach me, and I will be quiet; show me where I have
been wrong.

JOB 6:24 NIV

Show me your ways, O Lord, teach me your paths; guide
me in your truth and teach me, for you are God my
Savior, and my hope is in you all day long. . . . He guides
the humble in what is right and teaches them his way.

PSALM 25:4–5, 9 NIV

—INSTRUCTIONS FOR YOUR CHILD—

Don't sin by letting anger control you. Don't let the sun go down while you are still angry, for anger gives a mighty foothold to the devil. . . . And do not bring sorrow to God's Holy Spirit by the way you live. . . . Be kind to each other, tenderhearted, forgiving one another, just as God through Christ has forgiven you.

EPHESIANS 4:26–27, 30–32 NLT

In everything, therefore, treat people the same way you want them to treat you.

MATTHEW 7:12 NASB

God blesses those people who are merciful. They will be treated with mercy!

MATTHEW 5:7 CEV

— EXAMPLES —

The older brother of the Prodigal Son is a classic example of an offended son. The father listened, then quietly affirmed his love and concern:

Look, dear son, you have always stayed by me, and everything I have is yours. We had to celebrate this happy day. For your brother was dead and has come back to life! He was lost, but now he is found.

LUKE 15:31–32 NLT

When believers withdraw from Jesus, He offers His fellowship and waits patiently for the door to open:

I stand at the door and knock. If you hear my voice and open the door, I will come in, and we will share a meal together as friends. Those who are victorious will sit with me on my throne.

REVELATION 3:20–21 NLT

PLEASE HELP
ME PARENT
MY CHILD

What are some ways
I can encourage my child?

Gently encourage the stragglers, and reach out for the exhausted, pulling them to their feet. Be patient with each person, attentive to individual needs. . . . Look for the best in each other, and always do your best to bring it out.

1 THESSALONIANS 5:14–15 THE MESSAGE

— INSTRUCTIONS —

Say only what helps, each word a gift.

EPHESIANS 4:29 THE MESSAGE

Share each other's burdens, and in this way obey the law of Christ.

GALATIANS 6:2 NLT

Love . . . is ever ready to believe the best of every person, its hopes are fadeless under all circumstances.

1 CORINTHIANS 13:7 AMP

Never stop praying. . . . Always pray by the power of the Spirit.

EPHESIANS 6:18 CEV

— PROMISES —

The Lord God has given me his words of wisdom so
that I may know what I should say to all these weary
ones. Morning by morning he wakens me and opens my
understanding to his will.

ISAIAH 50:4 TLB

All praise to God, the Father of our Lord Jesus Christ.
God is our merciful Father and the source of all comfort.
He comforts us in all our troubles so that we can comfort
others. When others are troubled, we will be able to give
them the same comfort God has given us.

2 CORINTHIANS 1:3–4 NLT

— TO PRAY FOR YOUR CHILD —

May the God of hope fill you with all joy and peace as
you trust in him, so that you may overflow with hope by
the power of the Holy Spirit.

ROMANS 15:13 NIV

We pray for God's power to help you do all the good
things that you hope to do and that your faith makes you
want to do. Then . . . you will bring honor
to the name of our Lord Jesus, and he
will bring honor to you.

2 THESSALONIANS 1:11–12 CEV

—INSTRUCTIONS FOR YOUR CHILD—

Happy is the person who doesn't listen to the wicked. He doesn't go where sinners go. He doesn't do what bad people do. He loves the Lord's teachings. He thinks about those teachings day and night. He is strong, like a tree planted by a river. It produces fruit in season. Its leaves don't die. Everything he does will succeed.

PSALM 1:1–3 ICB

Be strong and courageous. Do not be afraid or terrified because of them, for the Lord your God goes with you; he will never leave you nor forsake you.

DEUTERONOMY 31:6 NIV

Ask, and it will be given to you; seek, and you will find; knock, and it will be opened to you. For everyone who asks receives, and he who seeks finds, and to him who knocks it will be opened.

MATTHEW 7:7–8 NKJV

Give all your worries to him, because he cares for you.

1 PETER 5:7 ICB

The Lord is faithful, and He will strengthen and protect you from the evil one.

2 THESSALONIANS 3:3 NASB

You are from God, little children, and have overcome them; because greater is He who is in you than he who is in the world.

1 JOHN 4:4 NASB

For I, the Lord your God, will hold your right hand, saying to you, "Fear not, I will help you."

ISAIAH 41:13 NKJV

The only temptations that you have are the temptations that all people have. But you can trust God. He will not let you be tempted more than you can stand. But when you are tempted, God will also give you a way to escape that temptation. Then you will be able to stand it.

1 CORINTHIANS 10:13 ICB

God began doing a good work in you. And he will continue it until it is finished when Jesus Christ comes again. I am sure of that.

PHILIPPIANS 1:6 ICB

— EXAMPLE —

Barnabas encouraged Saul when nobody else wanted to give him a chance:

When he [Saul] came to Jerusalem, he tried to join the disciples, but they were all afraid of him, not believing that he really was a disciple. But Barnabas took him and brought him to the apostles. He told them how Saul on his journey had seen the Lord and that the Lord had spoken to him, and how in Damascus he had preached fearlessly in the name of Jesus. So Saul stayed with them and moved about freely in Jerusalem, speaking boldly in the name of the Lord.

ACTS 9:26–28 NIV

Above all, I want to be sure my child knows you, Lord. What should I do?

Memorize these laws and think about them. . . . Teach them to your children. Talk about them all the time—whether you're at home or walking along the road or going to bed at night, or getting up in the morning.

DEUTERONOMY 11:18–19 CEV

If anybody asks why you believe as you do, be ready to tell him.

1 PETER 3:15 TLB

— PROMISES —

Put your entire trust in the Master Jesus. Then you'll live as you were meant to live—and everyone in your house included!

ACTS 16:31 THE MESSAGE

Commit your way to the Lord, trust also in Him, and He shall bring it to pass.

PSALM 37:5 NIV

—TO PRAY FOR YOUR CHILD—

For this reason, ever since I heard about your faith in the Lord Jesus and your love for all the saints, I have not stopped giving thanks for you, remembering you in my prayers. I keep asking that the God of our Lord Jesus Christ, the glorious Father, may give you the spirit of wisdom and revelation, so that you may know him better. I pray also that the eyes of your heart may be enlightened in order that you may know the hope to which he has called you, the riches of his glorious inheritance in the saints, and his incomparably great power for us who believe. That power is like the working of his mighty strength.

EPHESIANS 1:15–19 NIV

For this reason I kneel before the Father. . . . I pray that out of his glorious riches he may strengthen you with power through his Spirit in your inner being, so that Christ may dwell in your hearts through faith.

EPHESIANS 3:14, 16–17 NIV

—INSTRUCTIONS FOR YOUR CHILD—

God loved the world so much that he gave his only Son so that anyone who believes in him shall not perish [die] but have eternal life.

JOHN 3:16 TLB

If we say we have no sin, we are only fooling ourselves and refusing to accept the truth.

1 JOHN 1:8 NLT

But God demonstrates his own love for us in this: While we were still sinners, Christ died for us.

ROMANS 5:8 NIV

We have left God's paths to follow our own. Yet the Lord laid on him [Jesus] the sins of us all.

ISAIAH 53:6 NLT

Yes, when Christ died, he died to defeat the power of sin one time—enough for all time. He now has a new life, and his new life is with God. In the same way, you should see yourselves as being dead to the power of sin and alive with God through Christ Jesus.

ROMANS 6:10–11 ICB

How can a young man stay pure? By reading your Word and following its rules. . . . I have thought much about your words, and stored them in my heart so that they would hold me back from sin.

PSALM 119:9, 11 TLB

If you love me, you will obey my commands.

JOHN 14:15 NCV

From childhood you have known the Holy Scriptures, which are able to make you wise for salvation through faith which is in Christ Jesus.

2 TIMOTHY 3:15 NKJV

— FOR YOUR CHILD TO PRAY —

If you confess with your mouth that Jesus is Lord and believe in your heart that God raised him from the dead, you will be saved.

ROMANS 10:9 NLT

Take away my sin, and I will be clean. Wash me, and I will be whiter than snow.

PSALM 51:7 ICB

Blessed Lord, teach me your rules. . . . I will meditate upon them and give them my full respect. I will delight in them and not forget them. . . . Open my eyes to see wonderful things in your Word.

PSALM 119:12, 15–16, 18 TLB

— PROMISES FOR YOUR CHILD —

If anyone is in Christ, he is a new creation; old things have passed away; behold, all things have become new.

2 CORINTHIANS 5:17 NKJV

If we confess our sins to him, he is faithful and just to forgive us our sins.

1 JOHN 1:9 NLT

The Lord your God will always be at your side, and he will never abandon you.

DEUTERONOMY 31:6 CEV

God is working in you to make you willing and able to obey him.

PHILIPPIANS 2:13 CEV

Be faithful until death, and I will give you the crown of life.

REVELATION 2:10 NASB

How can I help my child reach his full potential?

No one can receive anything unless God gives it from heaven.

JOHN 3:27 NLT

Unless the Lord builds the house, its builders labor in vain.

PSALM 127:1 NIV

The things you planned for us no one can recount to you; were I to speak and tell them, they would be too many to declare.

PSALM 40:5 NIV

— INSTRUCTIONS —

We are fellow workmen—joint promoters, laborers together—with and for God.

1 CORINTHIANS 3:9 AMP

Devote yourselves to prayer with an alert mind and a thankful heart.

COLOSSIANS 4:2 NLT

Be an example . . . with your words, your actions, your love, your faith, and your pure life. . . . Continue to read the Scriptures to the people, strengthen them, and teach them. . . . Be careful in your life and in your teaching. If you continue to live and teach rightly, you will save both yourself and those who listen to you.

1 TIMOTHY 4:12–13, 16 NCV

— TO PRAY FOR YOUR CHILD —

I pray that you may prosper in every way and [that your body] may keep well, even as [I know] your soul keeps well and prospers.

3 JOHN 2 AMP

We constantly pray for you, that our God may deem and count you worthy of [your] calling and [His] every gracious purpose of goodness, and with power may complete in [your] every particular work of faith (faith which is that leaning of the whole human personality on God in absolute trust and confidence in His power, wisdom, and goodness).

2 THESSALONIANS 1:11–12 AMP

May the God of peace—who brought up from the dead the Lord Jesus . . . equip you with all you need for doing his will. May he produce in you, through the power of Jesus Christ, every good thing that is pleasing to him.

HEBREWS 13:20–21 NLT

—INSTRUCTIONS FOR YOUR CHILD—

You're blessed when you stay on course, walking steadily on the road revealed by God. You're blessed when you follow his directions, doing your best to find him. That's right—you don't go off on your own; you walk straight along the road he set.

PSALM 119:1–3 THE MESSAGE

This book of the law shall not depart from your mouth, but you shall meditate on it day and night, so that you may be careful to do according to all that is written in it; for then you will make your way prosperous, and then you will have success.

JOSHUA 1:8 NASB

Be strong and do not give up, for your work will be rewarded.

2 CHRONICLES 15:7 NIV

No matter how much you want, laziness won't help a bit, but hard work will reward you with more than enough.

PROVERBS 13:4 CEV

Plans fail for lack of counsel, but with many advisers they succeed.

PROVERBS 15:22 NIV

If you do your job well, you will work for a ruler and never be a slave.

PROVERBS 22:29 CEV

Anyone too lazy to cook will starve, but a hard worker is a valuable treasure.

PROVERBS 12:27 CEV

— PROMISES FOR YOUR CHILD —

"For I know the plans I have for you," declares the Lord, "plans to prosper you and not to harm you, plans to give you hope and a future. Then you will call upon me and come and pray to me, and I will listen to you. You will seek me and find me when you seek me with all your heart."

JEREMIAH 29:11–13 NIV

We are God's workmanship, created in Christ Jesus to do good works, which God prepared in advance for us to do.

EPHESIANS 2:10 NIV

— EXAMPLE —

It is vital to your children's success that they know God will always be with them to fulfill His plans for them, and that they can discover God's plan by learning His Word. God told Joshua:

No one will be able to stand against you as long as you live. For I will be with you as I was with Moses. I will not

fail you or abandon you. . . . Study this Book of Instruction continually. Meditate on it day and night so you will be sure to obey everything written in it. Only then will you prosper and succeed in all you do. This is my command—be strong and courageous! Do not be afraid or discouraged. For the Lord your God is with you wherever you go.

JOSHUA 1:5, 8–9 NLT

God, is there any way I can help my child choose wholesome friends?

The Lord grants wisdom! His every word is a treasure of knowledge and understanding. He grants good sense to the godly—his saints. He is their shield, protecting them and guarding their pathway. He shows how to distinguish right from wrong, how to find the right decision every time.

PROVERBS 2:6–9 TLB

— PROMISES —

He who fears the Lord has a secure fortress, and for his children it will be a refuge.

PROVERBS 14:26 NIV

Oh, the joys of those who do not follow evil men's advice, who do not hang around with sinners, scoffing at the things of God.

PSALM 1:1 TLB

—TO PRAY FOR YOUR CHILD—

For wisdom will enter your heart, and knowledge will be pleasant to your soul; discretion will guard you, understanding will watch over you, to deliver you from the way of evil, from the man who speaks perverse things; from those who leave the paths of uprightness, to walk in the ways of darkness. . . . Whose paths are crooked, and who are devious in their ways. . . . So you will walk in the way of good men and keep to the paths of the righteous.

PROVERBS 2:10–13, 15, 20 NASB

—INSTRUCTIONS FOR YOUR CHILD—

[Your] decisions must be based upon my laws.

EZEKIEL 44:24 TLB

Run away from the evil desires of youth. Try hard to live right and to have faith, love, and peace, together with those who trust in the Lord from pure hearts.

2 TIMOTHY 2:22 NCV

I am a companion of all those who fear You, and of those who keep Your precepts.

PSALM 119:63 NASB

Wise friends make you wise, but you hurt yourself by going around with fools.

PROVERBS 13:20 CEV

Stay away from fools or you won't learn a thing. Wise people have enough sense to find their way, but stupid fools get lost. Fools don't care if they are wrong, but God is pleased when people do right.

PROVERBS 14:7–9 CEV

Friends come and friends go, but a true friend sticks by you like family.

PROVERBS 18:24 THE MESSAGE

Don't make friends with someone who easily gets angry. Don't spend time with someone who has a bad temper.

PROVERBS 22:24 ICB

You are not to associate with anyone who claims to be a believer yet indulges in sexual sin, or is greedy, or worships idols, or is abusive, or is a drunkard, or cheats people. Don't even eat with such people.

1 CORINTHIANS 5:11 NLT

Do not be deceived: "Bad company corrupts good morals."

1 CORINTHIANS 15:33 NASB

Stop forming inappropriate relationships with unbelievers. Can right and wrong be partners? Can light have anything in common with darkness? Can Christ agree with the devil? Can a believer share life with an unbeliever? Can God's temple contain false Gods? Clearly we are the temple of the living God.

2 CORINTHIANS 6:14–16 GWT

— PROMISES FOR YOUR CHILD —

Blessed is the person who does not follow the advice of wicked people, take the path of sinners, or join the company of mockers. Rather, he delights in the teachings of the Lord and reflects on his teachings day and night. He is like a tree planted beside streams—a tree that produces fruit in season and whose leaves do not wither. He succeeds in everything he does.

PSALM 1:1–3 GWT

From childhood you have been acquainted with the sacred writings, which are able to make you wise for salvation through faith in Christ Jesus.

2 TIMOTHY 3:15 ESV

Wisdom will control your mind, and you will be pleased with knowledge. Sound judgment and good sense will watch over you.

PROVERBS 2:10–11 CEV

— EXAMPLE —

The Lord declared He would put a "hedge of protection" around Gomer to cut her off from evil friends:

I will block her road with thornbushes. I will build a wall around her so she cannot find her way. . . . She will look for them. But she won't find them.

HOSEA 2:6–7 ICB

How can I help my children with peer pressure and teach them to stand alone when necessary?

Direct your children onto the right path, and when they are older, they will not leave it.

PROVERBS 22:6 NLT

— INSTRUCTION —

Speak up for the right living that goes along with true Christianity. . . . Urge [your] young . . . to behave carefully, taking life seriously. And here you yourself must be an example to them of good deeds of every kind. Let everything you do reflect your love of the truth and the fact that you are in dead earnest about it.

TITUS 2:1, 6–7 TLB

— PROMISE —

The Lord who made you and helps you says: Do not be afraid . . . my chosen one . . . I will pour out my Spirit on your descendants, and my blessing on your children.

They will thrive like watered grass, like willows on a riverbank.

ISAIAH 44:2–4 NLT

— TO PRAY FOR YOUR CHILD —

For this [child] I prayed, and the Lord has given me my petition which I asked of Him. So I have also dedicated him to the Lord; as long as he lives he is dedicated to the Lord.

1 SAMUEL 1:27–28 NASB

I have given them your word. And the world hates them because they do not belong to the world, just as I do not. I'm not asking you to take them out of the world, but to keep them safe from the evil one. They are not part of this world any more than I am. Make them pure and holy by teaching them your words of truth. As you sent me into the world, I am sending them into the world. And I give myself entirely to you so they also might be entirely yours.

JOHN 17:14–19 NLT

May the God of peace himself make you entirely pure and devoted to God; and may your spirit and soul and body be kept strong and blameless until that day when our Lord Jesus Christ comes back again.

1 THESSALONIANS 5:23 TLB

—INSTRUCTIONS FOR YOUR CHILD—

Ask the Lord Jesus Christ to help you live as you should, and don't make plans to enjoy evil.

ROMANS 13:14 TLB

Do not follow the crowd in doing wrong.

EXODUS 23:2 NIV

Don't sin because others do, but stay close to God.

1 TIMOTHY 5:22 CEV

Keep yourself pure.

1 TIMOTHY 5:22 NKJV

Put on the full armor of God, so that when the day of evil comes, you may be able to stand your ground.

EPHESIANS 6:13 NIV

Run from temptations that capture young people. Always do the right thing.

2 TIMOTHY 2:22 CEV

The common bond of rebels is their guilt. The common bond of godly people is good will.

PROVERBS 14:9 TLB

Don't follow the ways of the wicked. Don't do what evil people do. Avoid their ways. Don't go near what they do.

Stay away from them and keep on going. They cannot sleep until they do evil. They cannot rest until they hurt someone. They fill themselves with wickedness and cruelty as if they were eating bread and drinking wine. The way of the good person is like the light of dawn. It grows brighter and brighter until it is full daylight. But the wicked are like those who stumble in the dark. They can't even see what has hurt them.

PROVERBS 4:14–19 ICB

If young toughs tell you, "Come and join us"—turn your back on them! "We'll hide and rob and kill," they say. "Good or bad, we'll treat them all alike. And the loot we'll get! All kinds of stuff! Come on, throw in your lot with us; we'll split with you in equal shares." Don't do it, son! Stay far from men like that, for crime is their way of life, and murder is their specialty. They will die a violent death.

PROVERBS 1:10–16, 19 TLB

God blesses those people who are treated badly for doing right. They belong to the kingdom of heaven. God will bless you when people insult you, mistreat you, and tell all kinds of evil lies about you because of me. Be happy and excited! You will have a great reward in heaven. People did these same things to the prophets who lived long ago.

MATTHEW 5:10–12 CEV

— FOR YOUR CHILD TO PRAY —

How can a young person live a pure life? He can do it by obeying your word. With all my heart I try to obey you, God. Don't let me break your commands. I have taken your words to heart so I would not sin against you. Lord, you should be praised. Teach me your demands.

PSALM 119:9–12 ICB

Lord, defend me. I have lived an innocent life. I trusted the Lord and never doubted. Lord, try me and test me. Look closely into my heart and mind. I see your love. I live by your truth. I do not spend time with liars. I do not make friends with people who hide their sin. I hate the company of evil people. I have lived an innocent life. . . . So save me and be kind to me.

PSALM 26:1–5, 11 ICB

The Lord is my light and my salvation; whom shall I fear? The Lord is the strength of my life; of whom shall I be afraid?

PSALM 27:1 NKJV

If God is for us, who can be against us?

ROMANS 8:31 NKJV

— EXAMPLES —

Shadrach, Meshach, and Abednego stood together against tremendous pressure. Because they steadfastly refused to bow down and worship the golden idol, God protected and promoted them:

The fire hadn't touched them—not a hair of their heads was singed; their coats were unscorched, and they didn't even smell of smoke! Then Nebuchadnezzar said, "Blessed be the God of Shadrach, Meshach, and Abednego, for he sent his angel to deliver his trusting servants when they defied the king's commandment and were willing to die rather than serve or worship any god except their own." . . . Then the king gave promotions to Shadrach, Meshach, and Abednego, so that they prospered greatly there in the province of Babylon.

DANIEL 3:27–28, 30 TLB

Moses also chose to side with God instead of with the people around him:

By faith Moses, when he had grown up, refused to be known as the son of Pharaoh's daughter. He chose to be mistreated along with the people of God rather than to enjoy the pleasures of sin for a short time.

HEBREWS 11:24–25 NIV

Because of his faith, Moses left Egypt. Moses had seen the invisible God and wasn't afraid of the king's anger.

HEBREWS 11:27 CEV

How can I teach my child the value of honesty?

Be an example . . . with your words, your actions, your love, your faith, and your pure life.

1 TIMOTHY 4:12 NCV

We have always lived honestly and sincerely, especially when we were with you. And we were guided by God's wonderful kindness instead of by the wisdom of this world. . . . God can be trusted, and so can I.

2 CORINTHIANS 1:12, 18 CEV

— INSTRUCTIONS —

Be careful, and watch yourselves closely so that you do not forget the things your eyes have seen or let them slip from your heart as long as you live. Teach them to your children and to their children after them.

DEUTERONOMY 4:9 NIV

God-loyal people, living honest lives, make it much easier for their children.

PROVERBS 20:7 THE MESSAGE

—TO PRAY FOR YOUR CHILD—

We have continued praying for you, asking God that you will know fully what he wants. We pray that you will also have great wisdom and understanding in spiritual things so that you will live the kind of life that honors and pleases the Lord in every way. . . . God has freed us from the power of darkness, and he brought us into the kingdom of his dear Son.

COLOSSIANS 1:9–10, 13 NCV

—INSTRUCTIONS FOR YOUR CHILD—

Lovingly follow the truth at all times—speaking truly, dealing truly, living truly—and so become more and more in every way like Christ.

EPHESIANS 4:15 TLB

You must stop telling lies. Tell each other the truth, because we all belong to each other in the same body.

EPHESIANS 4:25 NCV

He who walks in uprightness reverently and worship-fully fears the Lord, but he who is contrary and devious in his ways despises Him.

PROVERBS 14:2 AMP

Avoid all perverse talk; stay away from corrupt speech.

PROVERBS 4:24 NLT

Do not lie to each other. You have left your old sinful life and the things you did before. You have begun to live the new life, in which you are being made new and are becoming like the One who made you. This new life brings you the true knowledge of God.

COLOSSIANS 3:9–10 NCV

Truthful lips will be established forever, but a lying tongue is only for a moment.

PROVERBS 12:19 NASB

Dishonest witnesses and liars will be destroyed.

PROVERBS 19:9 CEV

Honesty guides good people; dishonesty destroys treacherous people.

PROVERBS 11:3 NLT

Liars have lied so well and for so long that they've lost their capacity for truth.

1 TIMOTHY 4:2 THE MESSAGE

— PROMISES FOR YOUR CHILD —

Do you want to live and enjoy a long life? Then don't say cruel things and don't tell lies. Do good instead of evil and try to live at peace. If you obey the Lord, he will watch over you and answer your prayers. But God despises evil people, and he will wipe them from the earth, till they are forgotten. When his people pray for help, he listens and rescues them from their troubles.

PSALM 34:12–17 CEV

If anyone is in Christ, he is a new creation; the old has gone, the new has come!

2 CORINTHIANS 5:17 NIV

It is God who works in you, both to will and to work for his good pleasure.

PHILIPPIANS 2:13 ESV

— FOR YOUR CHILD TO PRAY —

Create in me a new, clean heart, O God, filled with clean thoughts and right desires.

PSALM 51:10 TLB

You want me to be completely truthful. So teach me wisdom. Take away my sin, and I will be clean. Wash me, and I will be whiter than snow.

PSALM 51:6–7 ICB

— EXAMPLES —

There are many accounts in the Bible of people telling lies. Lies always bring consequences:

Then [Peter] began to curse and swear, "I do not know the man!" And immediately a rooster crowed. And Peter remembered the word which Jesus had said, "Before a rooster crows, you will deny Me three times." And he went out and wept bitterly.

MATTHEW 26:74–75 NASB

Now he went in and stood before his master. Elisha said to him, "Where did you go, Gehazi?" And he said, "Your servant did not go anywhere." Then he said to him, "Did not my heart go with you when the man turned back from his chariot to meet you? Is it time to receive money and to receive clothing, olive groves and vineyards, sheep and oxen, male and female servants? Therefore the leprosy of Naaman shall cling to you and your descendants forever." And he went out from his presence leprous, as white as snow.

2 KINGS 5:25–27 NKJV

About three hours later his wife came in, not knowing what had happened. Peter asked her, "Tell me, is this the price you and Ananias got for the land?" "Yes," she said, "that is the price." Peter said to her, "How could you agree to test the Spirit of the Lord? Look! The feet of the men who buried your husband are at the door, and they will carry you out also." At that moment she fell down at his feet and died.

ACTS 5:7–10 NIV

What can I do about sibling rivalry?

Promote the kind of living that reflects right teaching. . . . Encourage the young men to live wisely in all they do. And you yourself must be an example to them by doing good deeds of every kind. Let everything you do reflect the integrity and seriousness of your teaching.

TITUS 2:1, 6–8 NLT

— INSTRUCTIONS —

The Lord's servant must not quarrel; instead, he must be kind to everyone, able to teach, not resentful.

2 TIMOTHY 2:24 NIV

Submit to one another out of reverence for Christ. Children, obey your parents in the Lord, for this is right.

EPHESIANS 5:21; 6:1 NIV

Don't show favoritism.

JAMES 2:1 NIV

— PROMISES —

Correct your son, and he will give you rest; yes, he will give delight to your heart.

PROVERBS 29:17 AMP

All your . . . children shall be disciples—taught of the Lord [and obedient to His will]; and great shall be the peace and undisturbed composure of your children.

ISAIAH 54:13 AMP

It is written in the book of the prophets, and they shall all be taught of God—have Him in person for their teacher.

JOHN 6:45 AMP

— TO PRAY FOR YOUR CHILD —

May God give you more and more grace and peace as you grow in your knowledge of God and Jesus our Lord . . . with a generous provision of moral excellence . . . knowledge with self-control, and self-control with patient endurance, and patient endurance with godliness.

2 PETER 1:2, 5–6 NLT

Now may the God of peace who brought up our Lord Jesus from the dead . . . make you complete in every good work to do His will, working in you what is well pleasing in His sight, through Jesus Christ.

HEBREWS 13:20–21 NKJV

— INSTRUCTIONS FOR YOUR CHILD —

Whatever you desire that others would do to and for you, even so do also to and for them.

MATTHEW 7:12 AMP

Everyone should be quick to listen, slow to speak, and should not get angry easily.

JAMES 1:19 GWT

Do nothing from selfishness or empty conceit, but with humility of mind regard one another as more important than yourselves; do not merely look out for your own personal interests, but also for the interests of others.

PHILIPPIANS 2:3–4 NASB

Don't use bad language. Say only what is good and helpful to those you are talking to.

EPHESIANS 4:29 TLB

A gentle response defuses anger, but a sharp tongue kindles a temper-fire.

PROVERBS 15:1 THE MESSAGE

Let all bitterness and wrath and anger and clamor and slander be put away from you, along with all malice. Walk in love, as Christ loved us and gave himself up for us.

EPHESIANS 4:31–5:2 ESV

For the whole law can be summed up in this one command: "Love your neighbor as yourself." But if instead of showing love among yourselves you are always biting and devouring one another, watch out! Beware of destroying one another.

GALATIANS 5:14–15 NLT

Do you know where your fights and arguments come from? They come from the selfish desires that make war inside you. You want things, but you do not have them. So you are ready to kill and are jealous of other people. But you still cannot get what you want. So you argue and fight. You do not get what you want because you do not ask God.

JAMES 4:1–2 ICB

Let the peace of Christ keep you in tune with each other, in step with each other. None of this going off and doing your own thing. And cultivate thankfulness.

COLOSSIANS 3:15 THE MESSAGE

Do not do wrong to a person to pay him back for doing wrong to you. Or do not insult someone to pay him back for insulting you. But ask God to bless that person. Do this, because you yourselves were called to receive a blessing. . . . If you are always trying to do good, no one can really hurt you.

1 PETER 3:9, 13 ICB

— PROMISES FOR YOUR CHILD —

When [we are] pleasing to the Lord, He makes even [our] enemies to be at peace with [us].

PROVERBS 16:7 NASB

Peacemakers will plant seeds of peace and reap a harvest of goodness.

JAMES 3:18 NLT

The eyes of the Lord watch over those who do right, and his ears are open to their prayers. But the Lord turns his face against those who do evil.

1 PETER 3:11–12 NLT

—FOR YOUR CHILD TO PRAY—

Love your enemies. Pray for those who hurt you. If you do this, then you will be true sons of your Father in heaven.

MATTHEW 5:44–45 ICB

Here are some examples of that type of prayer:

Jesus said, "Father, forgive them. They don't know what they are doing."

LUKE 23:34 ICB

He [Stephen] fell on his knees and cried out, "Lord, do not hold this sin against them."

ACTS 7:60 NIV

—EXAMPLES—

Rebekah told her son Jacob to deceive his father in order to receive the blessing that rightfully belonged to his brother Esau:

So Esau hated Jacob because of the blessing that his father had given him.

GENESIS 27:41 GWT

Beware of showing favoritism to your children. Tremendous damage to a family can result:

Now as it happened, Israel loved Joseph more than any of his other children, because Joseph was born to him in his old age. So one day Jacob gave him a special gift— a brightly colored coat. His brothers of course noticed their father's partiality, and consequently hated Joseph; they couldn't say a kind word to him.

GENESIS 37:3–4 TLB

My child is sick.
What can I do?

He who fears the Lord has a secure fortress, and for his children it will be a refuge.

PROVERBS 14:26 NIV

"Because he loves me," says the Lord, "I will rescue him; I will protect him, for he acknowledges my name. He will call upon me, and I will answer him; I will be with him in trouble, I will deliver him and honor him. With long life will I satisfy him and show him my salvation."

PSALM 91:14–16 NIV

— INSTRUCTIONS —

Is any one of you sick? He should call the elders of the church to pray over him and anoint him with oil in the name of the Lord. And the prayer offered in faith will make the sick person well; the Lord will raise him up.

JAMES 5:14–15 NIV

These signs will accompany those who believe . . . they will place their hands on sick people, and they will get well.

MARK 16:17–18 NIV

[Jesus said] I will do whatever you ask in my name.

JOHN 14:13 NIV

His salvation extends to the children's children of those who are faithful to his covenant, of those who obey his commandments!

PSALM 103:17–18 NLT

Give thanks to the Lord and proclaim his greatness. Let the whole world know what he has done. Sing to him; yes, sing his praises. Tell everyone about his wonderful deeds. Rejoice, you who worship the Lord!

PSALM 105:1–3 NLT

O my soul, bless God, don't forget a single blessing! He forgives your sins—every one. He heals your diseases—every one.

PSALM 103:2–3 THE MESSAGE

What shall I render to the Lord for all His benefits toward me? I will take up the cup of salvation, and call upon the name of the Lord. . . . I will offer to You the sacrifice of thanksgiving, and will call upon the name of the Lord.

PSALM 116:12–13, 17 NKJV

Never give up praying.

COLOSSIANS 4:2 CEV

— PROMISES —

He is the faithful God who keeps his covenant for a
thousand generations and constantly loves those who
love him and obey his commands. . . . He will love you
and bless you. . . . And the Lord will protect you from all
sickness.

DEUTERONOMY 7:9, 13, 15 NLT

Our children too shall serve him, for they shall hear
from us about the wonders of the Lord; generations yet
unborn shall hear of all the miracles he did for us.

PSALM 22:30–31 TLB

— TO PRAY FOR YOUR CHILD —

Now may the God of peace Himself sanctify you
entirely; and may your spirit and soul and body be preserved complete, without blame at the coming of our
Lord Jesus Christ.

1 THESSALONIANS 5:23–24 NASB

He will cover you with his feathers, and under his wings
you will find refuge.

PSALM 91: 4 NIV

> May the God of Jacob keep you from all harm.
> May there be shouts of joy when we hear the
> news of your victory . . . praise to God for
> all that he has done for you.
> PSALM 20:1, 5 TLB

—INSTRUCTIONS FOR YOUR CHILD—

Pay attention, my child, to what I say. Listen carefully. Don't lose sight of my words. Let them penetrate deep within your heart, for they bring life and radiant health to anyone who discovers their meaning.

PROVERBS 4:20–22 NLT

Trust in the Lord with all your heart and do not lean on your own understanding. In all your ways acknowledge Him, and He will make your paths straight. Do not be wise in your own eyes; fear the Lord and turn away from evil. It will be healing to your body and refreshment to your bones.

PROVERBS 3:5–8 NASB

—PROMISES FOR YOUR CHILD—

"I will restore you to health" . . . declares the Lord.

JEREMIAH 30:17 NIV

We saw his suffering. We thought God was punishing him. But he was wounded for the wrong things we did. . . . And we are healed because of his wounds.

ISAIAH 53:4–5 ICB

Christ carried our sins in his body on the cross. . . . And we are healed because of his wounds.

1 PETER 2:24 ICB

Jesus Christ never changes! He is the same yesterday, today, and forever.

HEBREWS 13:8 CEV

—FOR YOUR CHILD TO PRAY—

My whole being, praise the Lord. Do not forget all his kindnesses. The Lord forgives me for all my sins. He heals all my diseases.

PSALM 103:2–3 ICB

Lord, how you have helped me before! You took me safely from my mother's womb and brought me through the years of infancy. I have depended upon you since birth; you have always been my God.

PSALM 22:9–11 TLB

—EXAMPLES—

There are many examples in the Bible of parents asking for—and receiving—healing for their children. Here are two:

Someone in the crowd shouted, "Teacher, please do something for my son! He is my only child." . . . Jesus ordered the demon to stop. Then he healed the boy and gave him back to his father. Everyone was amazed at God's great power.

LUKE 9:38, 42–43 CEV

A Gentile woman . . . came to him, pleading, "Have mercy on me, O Lord, Son of David! For my daughter has a demon in her, and it is severely tormenting her."

He said to the woman, "I was sent only to help the people of Israel—God's lost sheep—not the Gentiles." But she came and worshiped him and pleaded again, "Lord, help me!"

"It isn't right to take food from the children and throw it to the dogs," he said.

"Yes, Lord," she replied, "but even dogs are permitted to eat crumbs that fall beneath their master's table."

"Woman," Jesus said to her, "your faith is great. Your request is granted." And her daughter was instantly healed.

MATTHEW 15:22, 24–28 NLT

How can I be sure my child is telling me the truth?

Ears to hear and eyes to see—both are gifts from the Lord.

PROVERBS 20:12 NLT

— INSTRUCTIONS —

Call to me and I will answer you and tell you great and unsearchable things you do not know.

JEREMIAH 33:3 NIV

There is nothing covered up that will not be revealed, and hidden that will not be known.

LUKE 12:2 NASB

The heart of the discerning acquires knowledge; the ears of the wise seek it out.

PROVERBS 18:15 NIV

Understanding a person's thoughts is as hard as getting water from a deep well. But someone with understanding can find the wisdom there.

PROVERBS 20:5 ICB

We know these things because God has revealed them to us by his Spirit, and his Spirit searches out everything.

1 CORINTHIANS 2:10 NLT

Trust in the Lord with all your heart and do not lean on your own understanding. In all your ways acknowledge Him, and He will make your paths straight.

PROVERBS 3:5–6 NASB

Woe to those who go to great depths to hide their plans from the Lord, who do their work in darkness and think, "Who sees us? Who will know?"

ISAIAH 29:15 NIV

But when He, the Spirit of truth, comes, He will guide you into all the truth.

JOHN 16:13 NASB

He will bring to light what is hidden in darkness and will expose the motives of men's hearts.

1 CORINTHIANS 4:5 NIV

— PRAYERS —

Send forth your light and your truth, let them guide me.

PSALM 43:3 NIV

I will praise the Lord, who counsels me; even at night my heart instructs me. I have set the Lord always before me. Because he is at my right hand, I will not be shaken.

PSALM 16:7–8 NIV

— EXAMPLE —

When God revealed the king's dream to Daniel in a vision, the king fell on his face and said:

Surely your God is the God of gods and the Lord of kings and a revealer of mysteries, for you were able to reveal this mystery.

DANIEL 2:47 NIV

My child has walked away from you. I fear the consequences of his lifestyle.

I give you peace, the kind of peace that only I can give. It isn't like the peace that this world can give. So don't be worried or afraid.

JOHN 14:27 CEV

Who is among you who [reverently] fears the Lord, who obeys the voice of His servant, yet who walks in darkness and deep trouble and has no shining splendor [in his heart]? Let him rely on, trust and be confident in the name of the Lord, and let him lean upon and be supported by His God.

ISAIAH 50:10 AMP

For the Lord God helps me; therefore have I not been ashamed or confounded; therefore have I set my face like a flint, and I know that I shall not be put to shame.

ISAIAH 50:7 AMP

I would have despaired unless I had believed that I would see the goodness of the Lord in the land of the living. Wait for the Lord; be strong and let your heart take courage; yes, wait for the Lord.

PSALM 27:13–14 NASB

— INSTRUCTIONS —

Be an example to the believers with your words, your actions, your love, your faith, and your pure life.

1 TIMOTHY 4:12 NCV

Stay away from foolish and stupid arguments, because you know they grow into quarrels. And a servant of the Lord must not quarrel but must be kind to everyone, a good teacher, and patient. The Lord's servant must gently teach those who disagree.

2 TIMOTHY 2:23–25 NCV

Take into your heart all My words which I will speak to you and listen closely. Go to . . . the sons of your people, and speak to them and tell them, whether they listen or not.

EZEKIEL 3:10–11 NASB

I urge, then, first of all, that requests, prayers, intercession and thanksgiving be made for everyone. . . . This is good, and pleases God our Savior, who wants all men to be saved and to come to a knowledge of the truth.

1 TIMOTHY 2:1, 3–4 NIV

Open their eyes so that they may turn from darkness to light and from the dominion of Satan to God, that they may receive forgiveness of sins and an inheritance among those who have been sanctified by faith in Me.

ACTS 26:18 NASB

Pray without ceasing.

1 THESSALONIANS 5:17 NKJV

Now this is the confidence that we have in Him, that if we ask anything according to His will, He hears us. And if we know that He hears us, whatever we ask, we know that we have the petitions that we have asked of Him.

1 JOHN 5:14–15 NKJV

Behold, I have given you authority to tread on serpents and scorpions, and over all the power of the enemy, and nothing will injure you.

LUKE 10:19 NASB

And I will give you the keys of the kingdom of heaven, and whatever you bind on earth will be bound in heaven, and whatever you loose on earth will be loosed in heaven.

MATTHEW 16:19 NKJV

— TO PRAY FOR YOUR CHILD —

I pray that the eyes of your heart may be enlightened.

EPHESIANS 1:18 NASB

We ask God to give you a complete understanding of what he wants to do in your [life], and we ask him to make you wise with spiritual wisdom.

COLOSSIANS 1:9 NLT

And may the God of peace Himself sanctify you through and through—that is, separate you from profane things, make you pure and wholly consecrated to God—and may your spirit and soul and body be preserved sound and complete [and found] blameless at the coming of our Lord Jesus Christ, the Messiah. Faithful is He who is calling you [to Himself] and utterly trustworthy, and He will also do it [that is, fulfill His call by hallowing and keeping you].

1 Thessalonians 5:23–24 amp

Now may the God of peace—[who is] the Author and the Giver of peace . . . Strengthen (complete, perfect) and make you what you ought to be, and equip you with everything good that you may carry out His will; [while He Himself] works in you and accomplishes that which is pleasing in His sight, through Jesus Christ.

Hebrews 13:20–21 amp

— PROMISES —

For thus says the Lord God, "Behold, I Myself will search for My sheep and seek them out. As a shepherd cares for his herd in the day when he is among his scattered sheep, so I will care for My sheep and will deliver them from all the places to which they were scattered on a cloudy and gloomy day. . . . "I will feed My flock and I will lead them to rest," declares the Lord God. "I will seek the lost, bring back the scattered, bind up the broken, and strengthen the sick."

Ezekiel 34:11–12, 15–16 nasb

I will lead the blind by ways they have not known, along unfamiliar paths I will guide them; I will turn the darkness into light before them and make the rough places smooth. These are the things I will do; I will not forsake them.

ISAIAH 42:16 NIV

I will not contend for ever, neither will I be angry always, for [were it not so] the spirit [of man] would faint and be consumed before Me, and [My purpose in] creating the souls of men would be frustrated. . . . I have seen his [willful] ways, but I will heal him; I will lead him also, and will recompense him and restore comfort to him and to those who mourn for him.

ISAIAH 57:16, 18 AMP

Therefore thus says the Lord . . . Jacob shall not then be ashamed, not then shall his face become pale [with fear and disappointment because of his children's degeneracy].

For when he sees his children [walking in the ways of piety and virtue], the work of My hands in his midst, they will revere My name; they will revere the Holy One of Jacob and reverently fear the God of Israel. Those who err in spirit will come to understanding, and those who murmur [discontentedly] will accept instruction.

ISAIAH 29:22–24 AMP

Thus says the Lord, In an acceptable and favorable time I have heard and answered you, and in a day of salvation I have

helped you; and I will preserve you . . . Saying to those who are bound, Come forth; to those who are in spiritual darkness, Show yourselves—come into the light.

Isaiah 49:8–9 amp

And you shall know—with an acquaintance and understanding based on and grounded in personal experience—that I am the Lord: for they shall not be put to shame who wait for, look for, hope for and expect Me. . . . For thus says the Lord, Even the captives of the mighty shall be taken away, and the prey of the terrible shall be delivered; for I will contend with him who contends with you, and I will give safety to your children and ease them.

Isaiah 49:23, 25 amp

For though the mountains should depart and the hills be shaken or removed, yet My love and kindness shall not depart from you, nor shall My covenant of peace and completeness be removed, says the Lord, Who has compassion on you. . . . And all your . . . children shall be disciples—taught of the Lord [and obedient to His will]; and great shall be the peace and undisturbed composure of your children.

Isaiah 54:10, 13 amp

— EXAMPLES —

God allows His children to make their own choices:

God wasn't at all pleased; but he let them do it their way, worship every new god that came down the pike—and live with the consequences.

ACTS 7:42 THE MESSAGE

The father of the Prodigal Son also allowed his child to learn from his own mistakes. He did not nag him or drag him back home, but prayerfully watched for his return, received him back without condemnation, and celebrated his change of heart:

While he was still a long way off, his father saw him and felt compassion for him, and ran and embraced him and kissed him. . . . The father said to his slaves . . . "Let us eat and celebrate; for this son of mine was dead and has come to life again; he was lost and has been found."

LUKE 15:20, 22–24 NASB

AS A YOUNG PERSON, I HAVE SOME QUESTIONS ABOUT RELATIONSHIPS

What should I do when friends pressure me to do wrong?

Be decent and true in everything you do so that all can approve of your behavior. Don't spend your time in wild parties and getting drunk or in adultery and lust and fighting or jealousy. But ask the Lord Jesus Christ to help you live as you should, and don't make plans to enjoy evil.

ROMANS 13:13–14 TLB

— INSTRUCTIONS —

Do not follow the crowd in doing wrong.

EXODUS 23:2 NIV

Do not share in the sins of others. Keep yourself pure.

1 TIMOTHY 5:22 NIV

Run from temptations that capture young people. Always do the right thing.

2 TIMOTHY 2:22 CEV

Put on the full armor of God, so that when the day of evil comes, you may be able to stand your ground.

EPHESIANS 6:13 NIV

Don't become partners with those who reject God. How can you make a partnership out of right and wrong? That's not partnership; that's war. Is light best friends with dark? . . . So leave the corruption and compromise; leave it for good. . . . Don't link up with those who will pollute you.

2 CORINTHIANS 6:14, 17 THE MESSAGE

Let there be no sex sin, impurity or greed among you. Let no one be able to accuse you of any such things. Dirty stories, foul talk and coarse jokes—these are not for you. Instead, remind each other of God's goodness and be thankful. You can be sure of this: The Kingdom of Christ and of God will never belong to anyone who is impure or greedy, for a greedy person is really an idol worshiper—he loves and worships the good things of this life more than God.

Don't be fooled by those who try to excuse these sins, for the terrible wrath of God is upon all those who do them. Don't even associate with such people. For though once your heart was full of darkness, now it is full of light from the Lord, and your behavior should show it!

EPHESIANS 5:3–8 TLB

And so, dear brothers, I plead with you to give your bodies to God. Let them be a living sacrifice, holy—the kind he can accept. When you think of what he has done for you, is this too much to ask?

ROMANS 12:1 TLB

If a godly man compromises with the wicked, it is like
polluting a fountain or muddying a spring.

PROVERBS 25:26 TLB

Keep away from every kind of evil.

1 THESSALONIANS 5:22 TLB

The fear of man brings a snare, but whoever leans on,
trusts in, and puts his confidence in the Lord is safe and
set on high.

PROVERBS 29:25 AMP

— PROMISES —

God blesses those people who are treated badly for
doing right. They belong to the kingdom of heaven. God
will bless you when people insult you, mistreat you,
and tell all kinds of evil lies about you because of me.
Be happy and excited! You will have a great reward in
heaven. People did these same things to the prophets
who lived long ago.

MATTHEW 5:10–12 CEV

I have not turned against him. I have not stopped
following him. . . . The Lord God helps me.
So I will not be ashamed. I will be deter-
mined. I know I will not be disgraced.

ISAIAH 50:5, 7 ICB

— PRAYERS —

With all my heart I have sought You; Do not let me
wander from Your commandments. Your word I have
treasured in my heart, that I might not sin against You.
Blessed are You, O Lord; teach me your statutes.

PSALM 119:10–12 NASB

Lord, defend me. I have lived an innocent life. I trusted
the Lord and never doubted. Lord, try me and test me.
Look closely into my heart and mind. I see your love.
I live by your truth. I do not spend time with liars. I do
not make friends with people who hide their sin. I hate
the company of evil people. . . . Save me and be kind
to me.

PSALM 26:1–5, 11 ICB

[You are my] light and my salvation; whom shall I fear?
[You are] the strength of my life; of whom shall I be
afraid?

PSALM 27:1 NKJV

— EXAMPLE —

*Moses chose to side with God instead of
with the people around him:*

By faith Moses, when he had grown
up, refused to be known as the son of
Pharaoh's daughter. He chose to be

mistreated along with the people of God rather than to enjoy the pleasures of sin for a short time.

HEBREWS 11:24–25 NIV

It was because he trusted God that he left the land of Egypt and wasn't afraid of the king's anger. Moses kept right on going; it seemed as though he could see God right there with him.

HEBREWS 11:27 TLB

What about when friends drink or take drugs? Or hang out with the wrong group?

Don't copy the behavior and customs of this world, but be a new and different person with a fresh newness in all you do and think. Then you will learn from your own experience how his ways will really satisfy you.

ROMANS 12:2 TLB

— INSTRUCTIONS —

Don't follow the ways of the wicked. Don't do what evil people do. Avoid their ways. Don't go near what they do. Stay away from them and keep on going. They cannot sleep until they do evil. They cannot rest until they hurt someone. They fill themselves with wickedness and cruelty as if they were eating bread and drinking wine.

The way of the good person is like the light of dawn. It grows brighter and brighter until it is full daylight. But the wicked are like those who stumble in the dark. They can't even see what has hurt them.

PROVERBS 4:14–19 ICB

Don't envy evil men but continue to reverence the Lord all the time, for surely you have a wonderful future ahead of you. . . . My son, be wise and stay in God's paths; don't carouse with drunkards and gluttons, for they are on their way to poverty.

PROVERBS 23:17–20 TLB

Be very, very careful never to compromise . . . for if you do, you will soon be following their evil ways.

EXODUS 34:12 TLB

The night is far gone, the day of his return will soon be here. So quit the evil deeds of darkness and put on the armor of right living, as we who live in the daylight should! Be decent and true in everything you do so that all can approve your behavior. Don't spend your time in wild parties and getting drunk or in adultery and lust, or fighting, or jealousy. But ask the Lord Jesus Christ to help you live as you should, and don't make plans to enjoy evil.

ROMANS 13:12–14 TLB

You are not to keep company with anyone who claims to be a brother Christian but indulges in sexual sins, or is greedy, or is a swindler, or worships idols, or is a drunkard, or abusive. Don't even eat lunch with such a person.

1 CORINTHIANS 5:11 TLB

Wine gives false courage; hard liquor leads to brawls; what fools men are to let it master them, making them reel drunkenly down the street!

PROVERBS 20:1 TLB

You know well enough from your own experience that there are some acts of so-called freedom that destroy freedom. Offer yourselves to sin, for instance, and it's your last free act. But offer yourselves to the ways of God and the freedom never quits.

ROMANS 6:15–16 THE MESSAGE

Don't drink too much wine, for many evils lie along that path; be filled instead with the Holy Spirit and controlled by him.

EPHESIANS 5:18 TLB

For you are God's temple, the home of the living God, and God has said of you, "I will live in them and walk among them, and I will be their God and they shall be my people." That is why the Lord has said, "Leave them; separate yourselves from them; don't touch their filthy things, and I will welcome you and be a Father to you, and you will be my sons and daughters."

2 CORINTHIANS 6:16–18 TLB

Be with wise men and become wise. Be with evil men and become evil.

PROVERBS 13:20 TLB

Young men who are wise obey the law; a son who is a member of a lawless gang is a shame to his father.

PROVERBS 28:7 TLB

The common bond of rebels is their guilt. The common bond of godly people is good will.

PROVERBS 14:9 TLB

Don't you realize that making friends with God's enemies—the evil pleasures of this world—makes you an enemy of God? I say it again, that if your aim is to enjoy the evil pleasure of the unsaved world, you cannot also be a friend of God.

JAMES 4:4 TLB

Stop loving this evil world and all that it offers you, for when you love these things you show that you do not really love God . . . This world is fading away, and these evil, forbidden things will go with it, but whoever keeps doing the will of God will live forever.

1 JOHN 2:15, 17 TLB

Of course, your former friends will be very surprised when you don't eagerly join them anymore in the wicked things they do, and they will laugh at you in contempt and scorn. But just remember that they must face the Judge of all, living and dead; they will be punished for the way they have lived.

1 PETER 4:4–5 TLB

Dear brothers, you are only visitors here. Since your real home is in heaven, I beg you to keep away from the evil pleasures of this world; they are not for you, for they fight against your very souls.

1 PETER 2:11 TLB

Before every man there lies a wide and pleasant road
that seems right but ends in death.

PROVERBS 14:12 TLB

Take no part in the worthless pleasures of evil and darkness, but instead, rebuke and expose them.

EPHESIANS 5:11 TLB

Speak up for the right living that goes along with true
Christianity. . . . And here you yourself must be an
example to them of good deeds of every kind. Let everything you do reflect your love of the truth and the fact
that you are in dead earnest about it.

TITUS 2:1, 7 TLB

Be an example to the believers with your words, your
actions, your love, your faith, and your pure life.

1 TIMOTHY 4:12 NCV

There's trouble ahead when you live only for the
approval of others, saying what flatters them, doing
what indulges them. Popularity contests are not truth
contests. . . . Your task is to be true, not popular.

LUKE 6:26 THE MESSAGE

Dear brothers, pattern your lives after mine and notice
who else lives up to my example. For I have told you
often before, and I say it again now with tears in my
eyes, there are many who walk along the Christian road

who are really enemies of the cross of Christ. Their future is eternal loss, for their god is their appetite: they are proud of what they should be ashamed of; and all they think about is this life here on earth. But our homeland is in heaven, where our Savior the Lord Jesus Christ is; and we are looking forward to his return from there.

PHILIPPIANS 3:17–20 TLB

— PROMISES —

The Lord grants wisdom! His every word is a treasure of knowledge and understanding. He grants good sense to the godly—his saints. He is their shield, protecting them and guarding their pathway. . . . He shows how to distinguish right from wrong, how to find the right decision every time.

PROVERBS 2:6–7, 9 TLB

The Lord . . . will bring to light what is hidden in darkness and will expose the motives of men's hearts.

1 CORINTHIANS 4:5 NIV

— PRAYERS —

Keep me out of their power. Preserve me from their violence, for they are plotting against me.

PSALM 140:4 TLB

You will show me the path of life; in Your presence is fullness of joy, at Your right hand there are pleasures for evermore.

PSALM 16:11 AMP

You are my hiding place from every storm of life; you even keep me from getting into trouble! You surround me with songs of victory.

PSALM 32:7 TLB

— EXAMPLE —

The people you spend time with can have a dramatic impact on your spiritual life, as King Solomon found out:

The Lord had said to the sons of Israel, "You shall not associate with them, nor shall they associate with you, for they will surely turn your heart away after their gods." Solomon held fast to these. . . . His wives turned his heart away. . . . His heart was not wholly devoted to the Lord his God, as the heart of David his father had been.

1 KINGS 11:2, 4 NASB

What about sex?
How far should I go?

Above all else, guard your affections. For they influence everything else in your life. Spurn the careless kiss of a prostitute. Stay far from her. Look straight ahead; don't even turn your head to look. Watch your step. Stick to the path and be safe. Don't sidetrack; pull back your foot from danger.

PROVERBS 4:23–27 TLB

Honor marriage, and guard the sacredness of sexual intimacy between wife and husband. God draws a firm line against casual and illicit sex.

HEBREWS 13:4 THE MESSAGE

— INSTRUCTIONS —

The commandment is a lamp, and the law a light; reproofs of instruction are the way of life, to keep you from the evil woman, from the flattering tongue of a seductress. Do not lust after her beauty in your heart, nor let her allure you with her eyelids. . . . Can a man take fire to his bosom, and his clothes not be burned? Can one walk on hot coals, and his feet not be seared?

PROVERBS 6:23–25, 27–28 NKJV

Sexual sin is never right: our bodies were not made for that but for the Lord, and the Lord wants to fill our bodies with himself. . . . Don't you realize that your bodies are actually parts and members of Christ? So should I take part of Christ and join him to a prostitute? Never! And don't you know that if a man joins himself to a prostitute she becomes a part of him and he becomes a part of her? For God tells us in the Scripture that in his sight the two become one person. But if you give yourself to the Lord, you and Christ are joined together as one person.

1 CORINTHIANS 6:13, 15–17 TLB

That is why I say to run from sex sin. No other sin affects the body as this one does. When you sin this sin it is against your own body. Haven't you yet learned that your body is the home of the Holy Spirit God gave you, and that he lives within you? Your own body does not belong to you. For God has bought you with a great price. So use every part of your body to give glory back to God, because he owns it.

1 CORINTHIANS 6:18–20 TLB

Don't you realize that all of you together [the bride of Christ] are the temple of God and that the Spirit of God lives in you? God will destroy anyone who destroys this temple. For God's temple is holy, and you are that temple.

1 CORINTHIANS 3:16–17 NLT

Everyone who really believes this will try to stay pure because Christ is pure.

1 JOHN 3:3 TLB

Now you can have real love for everyone because your souls have been cleansed from selfishness and hatred when you trusted Christ to save you; so see to it that you really do love each other . . . with all your hearts.

1 PETER 1:22 TLB

Be an example . . . with your words, your actions, your love, your faith, and your pure life. . . . Continue to read the Scriptures to the people, strengthen them, and teach them. . . . Be careful in your life and in your teaching. If you continue to live and teach rightly, you will save both yourself and those who listen to you.

1 TIMOTHY 4:12–13, 16 NCV

Treat the older women as mothers, and the girls as your sisters, thinking only pure thoughts about them.

1 TIMOTHY 5:2 TLB

Avoid the very scenes of temptation.

PROVERBS 5:8 AMP

How can a young person live a pure life? He can do it by obeying your word. With all my heart I try to obey you, God. Don't let me break your commands.

PSALM 119:9–10 ICB

Abstain from all appearance of evil.

1 THESSALONIANS 5:22 KJV

If you notice that you are acting in ways inconsistent
with what you believe . . . then you know that you're
out of line. If the way you live isn't consistent with what
you believe, then it's wrong.

ROMANS 14:23 THE MESSAGE

— PROMISES —

Happy is the person who doesn't listen to the wicked.
He doesn't go where sinners go. He doesn't do what
bad people do. He loves the Lord's teachings. He thinks
about those teachings day and night. . . . Everything he
does will succeed.

PSALM 1:1–3 ICB

Every part of Scripture is . . . useful one way or
another—showing us truth, exposing our rebellion, correcting our mistakes, training us to live God's way.

2 TIMOTHY 3:16 THE MESSAGE

The eyes of the Lord watch over those who do right;
his ears are open to their cries for help. But the Lord
turns his face against those who do evil; he
will erase their memory from the earth.
The Lord hears his people when they
call to him for help. He rescues

them from all their troubles. . . . The Lord comes to the rescue each time.

PSALM 34:15–17, 19 NLT

Even if you think you can stand up to temptation, be careful not to fall. You are tempted in the same way that everyone else is tempted. But God can be trusted not to let you be tempted too much, and he will show you how to escape from your temptations.

1 CORINTHIANS 10:12–13 CEV

Now that the worst is over, we're pleased we can report that we've come out of this with conscience and faith intact, and can . . . face you with our heads held high. But it wasn't by any fancy footwork on our part. It was God who kept us focused on him, uncompromised.

2 CORINTHIANS 1:12 THE MESSAGE

God is working in you to make you willing and able to obey him.

PHILIPPIANS 2:13 CEV

— PRAYERS —

[Jesus prayed,] I have given them your word. And the world hates them because they do not belong to the world, just as I do not belong to the world. I'm not asking you to take them out of the world, but to keep them safe from the evil one. They do not belong to this world any more than I do. Make them holy by your truth; teach them your word, which is truth. Just as you sent me into the world, I am sending them into the world. And I give myself as a holy sacrifice for them so they can be made holy by your truth.

JOHN 17:14–19 NLT

When the skies are shut and there is no rain because of [my] sins, and then [I] pray . . . and claim you as [my] God, and turn from [my] sins . . . listen from heaven and forgive [my] sins . . . and teach [me] what is right.

2 CHRONICLES 6:26-27 TLB

To you, O Lord, I pray. . . . Show me the path where I should go, O Lord; point out the right road for me to walk. . . . Overlook my youthful sins, O Lord! Look at me instead through eyes of mercy and forgiveness.

PSALM 25:1, 4, 6 TLB

— EXAMPLE —

Joseph, a man of honor, refused to compromise his values and resisted the temptation to sexual sin:

It came about . . . that his master's wife looked with desire at Joseph, and she said, "Lie with me." But he refused and said . . . "How then could I do this great evil and sin against God?"

GENESIS 39:7–9 NASB

Now flee from youthful lusts and pursue righteousness, faith, love and peace, with those who call on the Lord from a pure heart.

2 TIMOTHY 2:22 NASB

What if things have already gone too far?

Remember this—the wrong desires that come into your life aren't anything new and different. Many others have faced exactly the same problems before you. And no temptation is irresistible. You can trust God to keep the temptation from becoming so strong that you can't stand up against it, for he has promised this and will do what he says. He will show you how to escape temptation's power so that you can bear up patiently against it.

1 CORINTHIANS 10:13 TLB

— INSTRUCTIONS —

Let the wicked forsake his way, and the unrighteous man his thoughts; let him return to the Lord, and He will have mercy on him; and to our God, for He will abundantly pardon.

ISAIAH 55:7 NKJV

I have set before you life and death, blessing and cursing; therefore choose life . . . that you may love the Lord your God, that you may obey His

voice, and that you may cling to Him, for He is your
life.

DEUTERONOMY 30:19–20 NKJV

He who conceals his sins does not prosper, but whoever
confesses and renounces them finds mercy.

PROVERBS 28:13 NIV

What happiness for those whose guilt has been forgiven!
What joys when sins are covered over! What relief for
those who have confessed their sins and God has cleared
their record. There was a time when I wouldn't admit
what a sinner I was. But my dishonesty made me miser-
able and filled my days with frustration. All day and all
night your hand was heavy on me. My strength evapo-
rated like water on a sunny day until I finally admitted
all my sins to you and stopped trying to hide them. I said
to myself, "I will confess them to the Lord." And you
forgave me! All my guilt is gone. Now I say that each
believer should confess his sins to God when he is aware
of them, while there is time to be forgiven. Judgment
will not touch him if he does. You are my hiding place
from every storm of life; you even keep me from getting
into trouble! You surround me with songs of victory.

PSALM 32:1–7 TLB

It is for freedom that Christ has set us free. Stand firm,
then, and do not let yourselves be burdened again by a
yoke of slavery. . . . So I say, live by the Spirit, and you
will not gratify the desires of the sinful nature.

GALATIANS 5:1, 16 NIV

If we walk in the Light as He Himself is in the Light, we have fellowship with one another, and the blood of Jesus His Son cleanses us from all sin. If we say that we have no sin, we are deceiving ourselves, and the truth is not in us.

1 JOHN 1:7–8 NASB

But if we confess our sins to him, he can be depended on to forgive us and to cleanse us from every wrong. (And it is perfectly proper for God to do this for us because Christ died to wash away our sins.)

1 JOHN 1:9 TLB

For his mercy toward those who fear and honor him is as great as the height of the heavens above the earth. He has removed our sins as far away from us as the east is from the west. He is like a father to us, tender and sympathetic to those who reverence him. For he knows we are but dust.

PSALM 103:11–14 TLB

Cling tightly to your faith in Christ, and always keep your conscience clear. For some people have deliberately violated their consciences; as a result, their faith has been shipwrecked.

1 TIMOTHY 1:19 NLT

Be self-controlled and alert. Your enemy the devil prowls around like a roaring lion looking for someone to devour. Resist him, standing firm in the faith.

1 PETER 5:8–9 NIV

Oh, wash me, cleanse me from this guilt. Let me be pure again.

PSALM 51:2 TLB

Have mercy on me, O God, according to your unfailing love; according to your great compassion blot out my transgressions. Wash away all my iniquity and cleanse me from my sin. For I know my transgressions, and my sin is always before me.

PSALM 51:1–3 NIV

Sprinkle me with the cleansing blood and I shall be clean again. Wash me and I shall be whiter than snow. And after you have punished me, give me back my joy again. Don't keep looking at my sins—erase them from your sight. Create in me a new, clean heart, O God, filled with clean thoughts and right desires. . . . Restore to me again the joy of your salvation, and make me willing to obey you.

PSALM 51:7–10, 12 TLB

Wash me, and I will be whiter than snow.

PSALM 51:7 ICB

Now may our Lord Jesus Christ Himself, and our God and Father, who has loved us . . . comfort your hearts and establish you in every good word and work. . . . The Lord is faithful, who will establish you and guard you from the evil one.

2 THESSALONIANS 2:16–17; 3:3 NKJV

— EXAMPLE —

Forgiveness requires repentance—you need to turn away from your sin and decide not to do it again:

The scribes and Pharisees brought to Him a woman caught in adultery. And when they had set her in the midst, they said to Him, "Teacher, this woman was caught in adultery, in the very act. Now Moses, in the law, commanded us that such should be stoned. But what do You say?"

He . . . said to them, "He who is without sin among you, let him throw a stone at her first."

Then those who heard it, being convicted by their conscience, went out one by one. . . . Jesus was left alone, and the woman standing in the midst. . . . He said to her, "Woman, where are those accusers of yours? Has no one condemned you?"

She said, "No one, Lord."

Jesus said to her, "Neither do I condemn you; go and sin no more."

JOHN 8:3–5, 7, 9–11 NKJV

Jesus forgives you, too. As you turn your heart away from your sin and choose to obey the Lord, He will help you and strengthen you in supernatural ways!

What's the best approach to dating?

Run from anything that gives you the evil thoughts that young men often have, but stay close to anything that makes you want to do right. Have faith and love, and enjoy the companionship of those who love the Lord and have pure hearts.

2 TIMOTHY 2:22 TLB

— INSTRUCTIONS —

Learn to put aside your own desires so that you will become patient and godly, gladly letting God have his way with you. This will make possible the next step, which is for you to enjoy other people and to like them, and finally you will grow to love them deeply.

2 PETER 1:6–7 TLB

Don't live to make a good impression on others. Be humble, thinking of others as better than yourself. Don't just think about your own affairs, but be interested in others, too, and in what they are doing.

PHILIPPIANS 2:3–4 TLB

Live no longer as the unsaved do, for they are blinded and confused. Their closed hearts are full of darkness; they are far away from the life of God because they have shut their minds against him, and they cannot understand his ways. They don't care anymore about right and wrong and have given themselves over to impure ways. They stop at nothing, being driven by their evil minds and reckless lusts.

EPHESIANS 4:17–19 TLB

Having such great promises as these, dear friends, let us turn away from everything wrong, whether of body or spirit, and purify ourselves, living in the wholesome fear of God, giving ourselves to him alone.

2 CORINTHIANS 7:1 TLB

— PROMISES —

Trust in the Lord with all your heart and do not lean on your own understanding. In all your ways acknowledge Him, and He will make your paths straight. Do not be wise in your own eyes; fear the Lord and turn away from evil.

PROVERBS 3:5–7 NASB

Delight yourself also in the Lord, and He shall give you the desires of your heart. Commit your way to the Lord, trust also in Him, and He shall bring it to pass. . . . Rest in the Lord, and wait patiently for Him.

PSALM 37:4–5, 7 NKJV

Seek first God's kingdom and what God wants. Then all your other needs will be met as well.

MATTHEW 6:33 NCV

— PRAYERS (BLESSINGS) —

May God who gives patience, steadiness, and encouragement help you to live in complete harmony with each other—each with the attitude of Christ toward the other.

And then all of us can praise the Lord together with one voice, giving glory to God, the Father of our Lord Jesus Christ.

ROMANS 15:5–6 TLB

May the God of peace himself make you entirely pure and devoted to God; and may your spirit and soul and body be kept strong and blameless until that day when our Lord Jesus Christ comes back again.

1 THESSALONIANS 5:23 TLB

My best friend won't talk to me. What should I do?

Always be willing to listen and slow to speak.

JAMES 1:19 NCV

—INSTRUCTIONS—

A kind answer soothes angry feelings, but harsh words stir them up.

PROVERBS 15:1 CEV

Listen carefully to what you hear! The way you treat others will be the way you will be treated.

MARK 4:24 CEV

Let the wise listen and add to their learning.

PROVERBS 1:5 NIV

The purposes of a man's heart are deep waters, but a man of understanding draws them out.

PROVERBS 20:5 NIV

Be happy with those who are happy, and weep with those who weep.

ROMANS 12:15 NLT

All of you should be of one mind. Sympathize with each other. Love each other as brothers and sisters. Be tender-hearted, and keep a humble attitude. Don't repay evil for evil. Don't retaliate with insults when people insult you. Instead, pay them back with a blessing. That is what God wants you to do, and he will bless you for it.

1 PETER 3:8–9 NLT

Let's agree to use all our energy in getting along with each other. Help others with encouraging words; don't drag them down by finding fault.

ROMANS 14:19 THE MESSAGE

Do not judge so that you will not be judged.

MATTHEW 7:1 NASB

Confess your sins to each other and pray for each other so that you can live together whole and healed. The prayer of a person living right with God is something powerful to be reckoned with.

JAMES 5:16 THE MESSAGE

He who covers his transgressions will not prosper, but whoever confesses and forsakes his sins shall obtain mercy.

PROVERBS 28:13 AMP

— PROMISES —

I will instruct you and teach you in the way you should go; I will counsel you and watch over you.

PSALM 32:8 NIV

Go, and I, even I, will be with your mouth, and teach you what you are to say.

EXODUS 4:12 NASB

— PRAYERS —

Teach me, and I will be quiet; show me where I have been wrong.

JOB 6:24 NIV

Show me your ways, O Lord, teach me your paths; guide me in your truth and teach me, for you are God my Savior, and my hope is in you all day long. . . . He guides the humble in what is right and teaches them his way.

PSALM 25:4–5, 9 NIV

— EXAMPLE —

When believers withdraw from Jesus, He offers His fellowship and waits patiently for the door to open:

Look! I stand at the door and knock. If you hear my voice and open the door, I will come in, and we will share a meal together as friends. Those who are victorious will sit with me on my throne.

REVELATION 3:20–21 NLT

CAN YOU HELP ME WITH THESE CHALLENGES?

I need to make a decision, Lord. How can I know what's best?

If you need wisdom, ask our generous God, and he will give it to you.

JAMES 1:5 NLT

— INSTRUCTIONS —

Call to me and I will answer you and tell you great and unsearchable things you do not know.

JEREMIAH 33:3 NIV

My son, if you accept my words and store up my commands within you, turning your ear to wisdom and applying your heart to understanding . . . and search for it as for hidden treasure, then you will understand the fear of the Lord and find the knowledge of God.

PROVERBS 2:1–2, 4–5 NLT

Trust God from the bottom of your heart; don't try to figure out everything on your own. Listen for God's voice in everything you do, everywhere you go; he's the one who will keep you on track. Don't assume that you know it all. Run to God!

PROVERBS 3:5–7 THE MESSAGE

All Scripture is inspired by God and is useful to teach us what is true and to make us realize what is wrong in our lives. It corrects us when we are wrong and teaches us to do what is right. God uses it to prepare and equip his people to do every good work.

2 TIMOTHY 3:16–17 NLT

— PROMISES —

I will instruct you and teach you in the way you should go; I will counsel you and watch over you.

PSALM 32:8 NIV

Your word is a lamp to my feet and a light to my path.

PSALM 119:105 NKJV

The statutes of the Lord are trustworthy, making wise the simple. The precepts of the Lord are right, giving joy to the heart. The commands of the Lord are radiant, giving light to the eyes. . . . By them is your servant warned; in keeping them there is great reward.

PSALM 19:7–8, 11 NIV

— PRAYERS —

Send forth your light and your truth, let them guide me.

PSALM 43:3 NIV

Show me the right path, O Lord; point out the road for me to follow. Lead me by your truth and teach me, for you are the God who saves me. All day long I put my hope in you.

PSALM 25:4–5 NLT

Teach me to do your will, for you are my God. May your gracious Spirit lead me forward on a firm footing.

PSALM 143:10 NLT

Give me an understanding mind so that I can govern your people well and know the difference between what is right and what is wrong. For who by himself is able to carry such a heavy responsibility?

1 KINGS 3:9 TLB

Your statutes are my delight; they are my counselors.

PSALM 119:24 NIV

— EXAMPLE —

When an enemy army came against Jehoshaphat, he sought the Lord for wisdom and guidance:

We have no power to face this vast army that is attacking us. We do not know what to do, but our eyes are upon you. . . . Then the Spirit of the Lord came upon

301

Jahaziel. . . . He said: "This is what the Lord says to you: 'Do not be afraid or discouraged because of this vast army. For the battle is not yours, but God's. . . . Go out to face them tomorrow, and the Lord will be with you.' "

2 CHRONICLES 20:12, 14–15, 17 NIV

Lord, I don't want to be a casual Christian. How can I bring your power into my world?

Put your mind on your life with God. The way to life—to God!—is vigorous and requires your total attention.

LUKE 13:24 THE MESSAGE

— INSTRUCTIONS —

Never be lacking in zeal, but keep your spiritual fervor, serving the Lord.

ROMANS 12:11 NIV

Don't let anyone think little of you because you are young. Be their ideal; let them follow the way you teach and live; be a pattern for them in your love, your faith, and your clean thoughts.

1 TIMOTHY 4:12 TLB

Soldiers don't get tied up in the affairs of civilian life, for then they cannot please the officer who enlisted them. And athletes cannot win the prize unless they follow the rules.

2 TIMOTHY 2:4–5 NLT

The seed planted in the good earth represents those who hear the Word, embrace it, and produce a harvest beyond their wildest dreams.

MARK 4:20 THE MESSAGE

Don't love the world's ways. Don't love the world's goods. Love of the world squeezes out love for the Father.

1 JOHN 2:15 THE MESSAGE

Practically everything that goes on in the world—wanting your own way, wanting everything for yourself, wanting to appear important—has nothing to do with the Father. It just isolates you from him. The world and all its wanting, wanting, wanting is on the way out—but whoever does what God wants is set for eternity.

1 JOHN 2:16–17 THE MESSAGE

God has given us different gifts for doing certain things well. So if God has given you the ability to prophesy, speak out with as much faith as God has given you. If your gift is serving others, serve them well. If you are a teacher, teach well. If your gift is to encourage others, be encouraging. If it is giving, give generously. If God has given you leadership ability, take the responsibility seriously. And if you have a gift for showing kindness to others, do it gladly.

ROMANS 12:6–8 NLT

To one is given the word of wisdom through the Spirit, to another the word of knowledge through the same Spirit, to another faith by the same Spirit, to another gifts of healings by the same Spirit, to another the working of miracles, to another prophecy, to another discerning of spirits, to another different kinds of tongues, to another the interpretation of tongues. But one and the same Spirit works all these things, distributing to each one individually as He wills.

1 Corinthians 12:8–11 nkjv

You will receive power when the Holy Spirit comes on you; and you will be my witnesses.

Acts 1:8 niv

Truly, truly, I say to you, he who believes in Me, the works that I do, will he do also; and greater works than these he will do; because I go to the Father. Whatever you ask in My name, that will I do, so that the Father may be glorified in the Son. If you ask Me anything in My name, I will do it.

John 14:12–14 nasb

— PRAYER —

Now the God of peace . . . equip you in every good thing to do His will, working in us that which is pleasing in His sight, through Jesus Christ, to whom be the glory forever and ever. Amen.

Hebrews 13:20–21 nasb

— EXAMPLE —

Jesus chose seventy of His followers and sent them out two by two ahead of Him to heal the sick and to proclaim that the kingdom of God has come:

Then the seventy returned with joy, saying, "Lord, even the demons are subject to us in Your name." And He said to them, "I saw Satan fall like lightning from heaven. Behold, I give you the authority . . . over all the power of the enemy, and nothing shall by any means hurt you."

LUKE 10:17–19 NKJV

All the same, the great triumph is not in your authority over evil, but in God's authority over you and presence with you.

LUKE 10:20 THE MESSAGE

Sometimes I feel like no one cares. Am I special to you, Lord?

Of all the people on earth, the Lord your God has chosen you to be his own special treasure. . . . He will love you and bless you.

    DEUTERONOMY 7:6, 13 NLT

Before I formed you in the womb I knew you, before you were born I set you apart.

    JEREMIAH 1:5 NIV

He pays . . . attention to you, down to the last detail— even numbering the hairs on your head!

    MATTHEW 10:29–30 THE MESSAGE

You know when I sit down or stand up. You know my thoughts even when I'm far away. . . . You know what I am going to say even before I say it, Lord. . . . You made all the delicate, inner parts of my body and knit me together in my mother's womb. . . . You saw me before I was born. Every day of my life was recorded in your book. Every moment was laid out before a single day had passed. How precious are your thoughts about me, O God. They cannot be numbered!

    PSALM 139:2, 4, 13, 16–17 NLT

You keep track of all my sorrows. You have collected all my tears in your bottle. You have recorded each one in your book.

PSALM 56:8 NLT

Long ago, even before he made the world, God chose us to be his very own. . . . His unchanging plan has always been to adopt us into his own family by sending Jesus Christ to die for us. And he did this because he wanted to!

EPHESIANS 1:4–5 TLB

Each of us is an original.

GALATIANS 5:26 THE MESSAGE

We are able to hold our heads high no matter what happens and know that all is well, for we know how dearly God loves us, and we feel this warm love everywhere within us because God has given us the Holy Spirit to fill our hearts with his love.

ROMANS 5:5 TLB

We know how much God loves us because we have felt his love and because we believe him when he tells us that he loves us dearly.

1 JOHN 4:16 TLB

— PROMISES —

God promises to love me all day, sing songs all through the night! My life is God's prayer.

PSALM 42:8 THE MESSAGE

When my father and my mother forsake me, then the Lord will take care of me.

PSALM 27:10 NKJV

— PRAYER —

May you be able to feel and understand, as all God's children should, how long, how wide, how deep, and how high his love really is; and to experience this love for yourselves, though it is so great that you will never see the end of it or fully know or understand it.

EPHESIANS 3:18–19 TLB

Lord, what if someone makes fun of me because I believe in you?

Fear not, for I am with you; be not dismayed, for I am your God. I will strengthen you, yes, I will help you, I will uphold you with My righteous right hand. Behold, all those who were incensed against you shall be ashamed and disgraced; they shall be as nothing.

ISAIAH 41:10–11 NKJV

Every word of God proves true. He defends all who come to him for protection.

PROVERBS 30:5 TLB

— INSTRUCTIONS —

Be an example to the believers with your words, your actions, your love, your faith, and your pure life.

1 TIMOTHY 4:12 NCV

[Jesus said,] You're blessed when your commitment to God provokes persecution. The persecution drives you even deeper into God's kingdom. Not only that— count yourselves blessed every time people put you down or throw you out or speak lies about you to discredit me. What it means is that the truth is too close for comfort and they are uncomfortable. You can be glad when that happens—give a cheer, even!—for though they don't like it, I do! And all heaven applauds. And know that you are in good company. My prophets and witnesses have always gotten into this kind of trouble.

MATTHEW 5:10–12 THE MESSAGE

[Paul said,] For I am not ashamed of the gospel of Christ, for it is the power of God to salvation for everyone who believes.

ROMANS 1:16 NKJV

This is why we work hard and continue to struggle, for our hope is in the living God, who is the Savior of all people.

1 TIMOTHY 4:10 NLT

Refuse foolish and ignorant speculations, knowing that they produce quarrels. The Lord's bond-servant must not be quarrelsome, but be kind to all, able to teach, patient when wronged, with gentleness correcting those who are in opposition, if perhaps God may grant them repentance leading to a knowledge of the truth.

2 TIMOTHY 2:23–25 NASB

If someone mistreats you because you are a Christian, don't curse him; pray that God will bless him.

ROMANS 12:14 TLB

Put on the full armor of God, so that when the day of evil comes, you may be able to stand your ground.

EPHESIANS 6:13 NIV

— PROMISES —

The good man does not escape all troubles—he has them too. But the Lord helps him in each and every one.

PSALM 34:19 TLB

You are of God, little children, and have overcome them, because He who is in you is greater than he who is in the world.

1 JOHN 4:4 NKJV

Fear of man will prove to be a snare, but whoever trusts in the Lord is kept safe.

PROVERBS 29:25 NIV

He Himself has said, "I will never leave you nor forsake you." So we may boldly say: "The Lord is my helper; I will not fear. What can man do to me?"

HEBREWS 13:5–6 NKJV

I give you peace, the kind of peace that only I can give. It isn't like the peace that this world can give. So don't be worried or afraid.

JOHN 14:27 CEV

— PRAYERS —

Lord, defend me. I have lived an innocent life. I trusted
the Lord and never doubted. Lord, try me and test me.
Look closely into my heart and mind. I see your love. I
live by your truth. I do not spend time with liars. I do not
make friends with people who hide their sin.

PSALM 26:1–4 ICB

The Lord is my light and my salvation; whom shall I
fear? The Lord is the strength of my life; of whom shall
I be afraid?

PSALM 27:1 NKJV

May the God of peace himself make you entirely pure
and devoted to God; and may your spirit and soul and
body be kept strong and blameless until that day when
our Lord Jesus Christ comes back again.

1 THESSALONIANS 5:23 TLB

— EXAMPLE —

*Shadrach, Meshach, and Abednego stood together
against tremendous pressure. Because they steadfastly
refused to bow down and worship the golden idol, God
protected and promoted them:*

The fire hadn't touched them—not a hair
of their heads was singed; their coats
were un-scorched, and they didn't even

smell of smoke! Then Nebuchadnezzar said, "Blessed be the God of Shadrach, Meshach, and Abednego, for he sent his angel to deliver his trusting servants when they defied the king's commandment, and were willing to die rather than serve or worship any god except their own." . . . Then the king gave promotions to Shadrach, Meshach, and Abednego, so that they prospered greatly there in the province of Babylon.

DANIEL 3:27–28, 30 TLB

Lord, everything seems so hopeless—I wish I could die. How can I go on?

"For I know the plans that I have for you," declares the Lord, "plans for welfare and not for calamity to give you a future and a hope. . . . You will seek Me and find Me when you search for Me with all your heart. I will be found by you . . . and I will restore your fortunes."

JEREMIAH 29:11, 13–14 NASB

Surely there is a future, and your hope will not be cut off.

PROVERBS 23:18 NASB

— PRAYERS —

O Lord, You have searched me and known me. You know my sitting down and my rising up; You understand my thought afar off. You comprehend my path and my lying down, and are acquainted with all my ways. For there is not a word on my tongue, but behold, O Lord, You know it altogether. . . . Such knowledge is too wonderful for me; it is high, I cannot attain it.

Where can I go from Your Spirit? Or where can I flee from Your presence? If I ascend into heaven, You are there; if I make my bed in hell, behold, You are there. If I take the wings of the morning, and dwell in the uttermost parts of the sea, even there Your hand shall lead me, and Your right hand shall hold me. . . .

How precious also are Your thoughts to me, O God! How great is the sum of them! If I should count them, they would be more in number than the sand; when I awake, I am still with You. . . . Lead me in the way everlasting.

PSALM 139:1–4, 6–10, 17–18, 24 NKJV

Whom have I in heaven but you? And earth has nothing I desire besides you. My flesh and my heart may fail, but God is the strength of my heart and my portion forever. . . . It is good to be near God. I have made the Sovereign Lord my refuge.

PSALM 73:25–26, 28 NIV

Though I walk in the midst of trouble, You will revive me; You will stretch out Your hand against the wrath of my enemies, and Your right hand will save me. The Lord will perfect that which concerns me; Your mercy, O Lord, endures forever.

PSALM 138:7–8 NKJV

[You have] said, "I will never leave you nor forsake you." So [I] may boldly say: "The Lord is my helper; I will not fear. What can man do to me?"

HEBREWS 13:5–6 NKJV

— EXAMPLE —

In the face of all his suffering, Job wanted to die. He felt like God and the universe were against him:

Oh, that I might have my request, and that God would grant me the thing that I long for! I even wish that it would please God to crush me; that He would let loose His hand and cut me off! . . . What strength have I left, that I should wait and hope? And what is ahead of me, that I should be patient?

JOB 6:8–9, 11 AMP

Fortunately, Job didn't give up too soon, since God had great plans for his future. God revealed himself to Job, then doubled his wealth and happiness:

I have heard of You [only] by the hearing of the ear; but now my [spiritual] eye sees You.

JOB 42:5 AMP

The Lord blessed Job at the end of his life more than at the beginning. . . . Job lived 140 years after that, living to see his grandchildren and great-grandchildren too. Then at last he died, an old, old man, after living a long, good life.

JOB 42:12, 16–17 TLB

BIBLE REFERENCES